Making Silver Chains

Making Silver Chains

Simple Techniques, Beautiful Designs

Glen F. Waszek

LARK BOOKS

A Division of Sterling Publishing Co., Inc.
New York

To Olga, whose foresight made it possible

Editor: Cindy Burda

Art Director and Production: Tom Metcalf

Production Assistant: Hannes Charen

Color photography: Evan Bracken

Black and white photography: Glen F. Waszek

Illustrations: Glen F. Waszek

Assistant Editors: Veronika Gunter and Catharine Sutherland

Editorial Intern: Emma Laurel Jones

Library of Congress Cataloging-in-Publication Data

Waszek, Glen.
   Making silver chains: simple techniques,
 beautiful designs/ by Glen Waszek.
      p.   cm.
   Includes index.
   ISBN 1-57990-183-2
     1. Jewelry making. 2. Chains (Jewelry) I. Title.

TT212. W38 2001
739.27'8—dc21
                        00-033098
                        CIP

Published by Lark Books, a division of
Sterling Publishing Co., Inc.
387 Park Avenue South, New York, N.Y. 10016
© 2001, Glen F. Waszek

Distributed in Canada by Sterling Publishing,
c/o Canadian Manda Group, One Atlantic Ave., Suite 105
Toronto, Ontario, Canada M6K 3E7

Distributed in the U.K. by:
Guild of Master Craftsman Publications Ltd., Castle Place 166 High street
Lewes, East Sussex, England BN7 1XU
Tel: (+ 44) 1273 477374 Fax: (+ 44) 1273 478606 Email: pubs@thegmcgroup.com
Web: www. gncpublications.com

If you have questions or comments about this book, please contact:
Lark Books
50 College St.
Asheville, NC 28801
(828) 253-0467
Printed in China
ISBN 1-57990-183-2

TABLE *of* CONTENTS

Introduction

Take a look around. Everyone's wearing jewelry! Funky beaded earrings, earthy woven bracelets, tasteful (and not so tasteful!) diamond rings. But no matter what other kinds of jewelry a person has, chances are he or she also has a few silver chains, too. Slim and simple or chunky and complex, they're the backbone of any jewelry collection. And a gorgeous handmade chain can be one of the showpieces.

Silver chains are surprisingly easy—and satisfying—to make. Yet when I first started making chains I couldn't find much of anything on the subject. The information that was available could be frustratingly vague—and worse still—discouraging. According to most sources, even making simple oval links required special equipment and materials. Nevertheless, I began experimenting with supplies I had on hand. And I'm pleased to tell you that you can make beautiful silver chains with equipment no more sophisticated than common finishing nails (which you'll use as mandrels—see page 19), an old house brick, and a basic torch.

Between a jewelry-supply store and your local hardware, you'll be able to find everything you need to make the chains in the following pages. That was one of the personal conditions I set when I decided to write this book. Another requirement was that only chains I've actually made be included. Perhaps the most important stipulation, however, was that the projects in the book be pleasing to wear. To me, a good chain should flow like water when pulled over the hand. If it doesn't feel good, it's a poor chain no matter how it looks.

Fortunately, I think you'll find that all the projects in here satisfy the eye, too. These are classic designs that never go out of style. My wife and daughter wear these chains all the time. And although my wife might wear them just because I made them, I can assure you that my daughter wouldn't put them on unless she was convinced they looked good on her!

Which answers the question, "Why make silver chains?" Whether you make one as a gift for a loved one, or as a special treat for yourself, a handmade chain is imbued with care and personal meaning that machine-made, store-bought jewelry simply can't match. It may seem that cutting and soldering large numbers of small links might take a lot of time. And to be sure, making a chain isn't a single-evening endeavor. However, these projects can usually be made over a weekend, and the results are well worth the effort! Years of pleasurable wear will reward your hours of work.

How to use this book

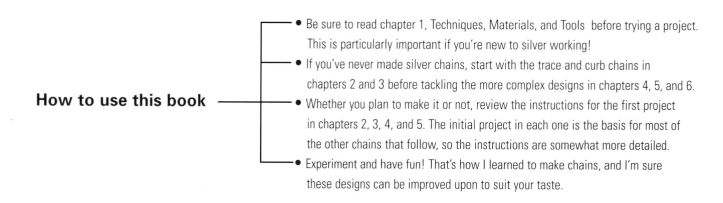

- Be sure to read chapter 1, Techniques, Materials, and Tools before trying a project. This is particularly important if you're new to silver working!
- If you've never made silver chains, start with the trace and curb chains in chapters 2 and 3 before tackling the more complex designs in chapters 4, 5, and 6.
- Whether you plan to make it or not, review the instructions for the first project in chapters 2, 3, 4, and 5. The initial project in each one is the basis for most of the other chains that follow, so the instructions are somewhat more detailed.
- Experiment and have fun! That's how I learned to make chains, and I'm sure these designs can be improved upon to suit your taste.

Gallery *of* projects

Below: The Teardrop-Link Chain (chapter 6, page 94) on the left is one of the most intricate designs in this book. On the right, the Tiny Oval-Link Trace Chain (chapter 2, page 42) is one of the most basic.

Above: One of the most attractive hand-made chains, the Triple Loop-in-Loop chain (chapter 5, page 81) is basically three single loop-in-loop chains woven together. The heavy, cordlike chain can be worn alone or with a special pendant.

Below: *A full twist of each link gives the Bow-Tie Link Chain (chapter 6, page 85) an elegant appearance.*

Above: *Two curb chains. To the left, the Basic Curb Chain (chapter 3, page 47) makes an attractive display for a favorite pendant. To the right, change a curb chain's looks by filing the tops of its links (chapter 3, page 53).*

Above: *Stylish and unusual, the Scalloped Necklace (chapter 6, page 102) is gorgeous on its own, without a pendant. Its length can be easily adjusted by adding to or subtracting from the plain oval links at either end.*

Below: *The Basic Trace Chain (chapter 2, page 35) forms a frame for the more complex Idiot's Delight Bracelet (chapter 4, page 65).*

Below: *They might not look much alike, but these are both curb chains. On the left, a Fetter-and-Three-Link Curb Chain (chapter 3, page 51). On the right, a very professional-looking curb chain with the tops and sides of its links filed (chapter 3, page 53).*

Above: *Looped together in a repeating pattern, simple round links become a delightful Wiggly Chain (chapter 4, page 66).*

10

Left: *On the left a variation of the loop-in-loop style, the links in the Foxtail Chain (chapter 5, page 76), look a little like the decorations that used to be seen hanging from car antennae. To the right, Figure-Eight Loops (chapter 6, page 91) form a graceful necklace.*

Right: *Changing the size and type of wire gives chains of the same style subtly different appearances. On the left, a Filed Curb Chain from Square Wire (chapter 3, page 56). On the right, a Small-Link Curb Chain (chapter 3, page 49).*

Above: *Using very heavy wire allows dramatic filing, completely transforming the wire's original round shape. Here, 12-gauge (2 mm) round silver wire makes a handsome Heavy-Link Filed Curb Bracelet (chapter 3, page 58).*

Left: *Weaving together large links of fine wire gives the Double Loop-in-Loop Chain (chapter 5, page 78) a rich, ropelike texture. Note how the attractive End Caps with a Hook and Ring fastener (chapter 7, page 109) adds an extra design element to this necklace.*

Below: *The stunning Double-Twisted Bow-Tie Link Chain (chapter 6, page 87) is a design not often found in jewelry stores; this unique chain is best made by hand.*

Left: *Handmade chains can have an almost machine-made perfection, as the Filed Curb Link Bracelet (chapter 3, page 55), on the left, shows; or, they can have a charming, homespun appearance, as with the Simple Twisted-Link Chain (chapter 6, page 84), to the right.*

Right: *The basic trace chain style offers a great deal of room for experimentation and variation. Here, the basic design takes on a whole new look when it's made with square wire. As you can see, a Trace Chain from Square Wire (chapter 2, page 39) has added sparkle and makes the perfect display for an uncomplicated pendant.*

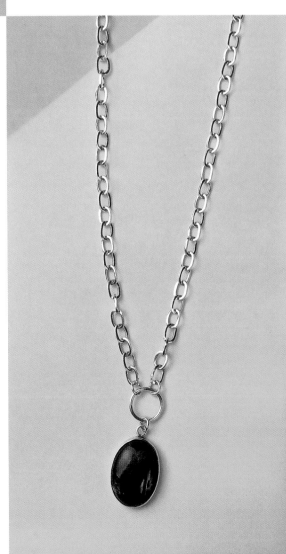

If you're new to working with silver, take a few minutes to read this chapter! Although it's not intended to replace a hands-on silver-working course, it does include all the basic information you'll need to make the projects in this book. Those of you who are presently making jewelry will probably already be familiar with most of the materials, tools, and techniques described here; however, because the information is presented in the sequence in which you'll use it when actually making chains, you may find the review useful.

The chapter will walk you through the basic processes of silver-working with easy-to-follow, step-by-step instructions. A complete materials and tools list proceeds each technique, and you'll find descriptions of any tools that might be unfamiliar.

Silver Wire

The most basic material for silver chain making is, of course, silver wire. I recommend sterling-silver wire for all of the projects in this book. *Sterling silver* is an alloy of $92\frac{1}{2}$ percent silver and $7\frac{1}{2}$ percent copper. You'll find sterling-silver wire at most jewelry-supply and craft stores. It's packaged in coils and sold by length. It's available in several styles, but the two used in this book are round and square wire.

Depending on where you live, the wire's diameter will be indicated in millimeters or by a Brown & Sharpe (B&S) gauge number. I made all of the chains shown in this book with wire sold in millimeter diameters. Unfortunately, as you can see in the chart below, B&S gauge numbers don't correspond exactly to millimeter sizes. If you use the B&S gauge suggested in the materials lists, rather than the millimeter diameter, your chains may look slightly heavier or lighter than those shown in the photos; however, they'll still be quite attractive. The only time you may need to make adjustments is when you're working with very small links or dense linkings. Then you may need to make the links slightly larger or adjust the length of the chain by adding or removing a link or two.

Periodically, you may need to check the diameter of a piece of wire, a task best handled with *vernier calipers*. (A ruler isn't accurate enough for the very small sizes involved in chain making.) You'll also use this tool to identify suitable *mandrels* (see pages 19 to 20) to form and shape links.

continued on page 16

Metric Wire Sizes and B&S Gauge "Equivalents"

Metric	Closest B&S Gauge	Actual B&S Size (mm)
2.00 mm	12	2.05 mm
1.50 mm	14	1.63 mm
1.25 mm	16	1.29 mm
1.00 mm	18	1.02 mm
0.75 mm	20	0.81 mm
0.64 mm	22	0.64 mm
0.50 mm	24	0.51 mm

As you can see, most of the conversions aren't exact. For the chains in chapters 2 and 3 the differences probably won't be noticeable. However, for the circular-link and loop-in-loop chains in chapters 4 and 5, the dimensions of the wire are more critical. Make a short test length of chain and, if necessary, adjust the mandrel sizes a little.

MATERIALS

Envelopes or small plastic bags

Fine-gauge binding wire made of iron

Flux for soldering

Flux for annealing

Forms (to coil wire around) for annealing

High-temperature solder

Liquid dish soap

Masking tape

Paper towels

Pickle granules

Pickle pot

Rubber gloves

Sandpaper, 400-grit and 800-grit

Self-pickling liquid flux

Steel tumbling shot

Sterling-silver wire

TOOLS

6-inch (15 cm) #2-cut hand file

Bamboo or copper tongs

Bench vise

Diagonal wire cutters

Hacksaw

Jeweler's-saw frame and #0 blades

Mandrels (each project lists the specific size[s] required)

Metal shears

Pliers:

    Two pairs of flat-nose pliers

    One pair of round-nose pliers

    Two pairs of chain-nose pliers

Small sable-hair artist's paintbrush

Soft-bristle artist's paintbrush

Soldering block

Tweezers:

    One pair of cross-locking tweezers

    One pair of third-hand cross-locking tweezers on a stand

    One pair of fine-tip tweezers

Torch and torch stand

Vernier calipers

If you've ever made jewelry, chances are you already own many of the tools and materials you'll need for chain making. The list on the left includes all of the standard items you should have on hand to make the projects in this book (Your local jewelry-supply or craft store should carry any you don't have.) Don't worry if any of these sound unfamiliar! This chapter covers what each one is and how and for what it's used.

Each one is described in this chapter under the technique(s) that require it. A few projects call for tools or materials that aren't on this list. When that happens, you'll see the special tool or material in the project's Materials and Tools list; most of these items are also described in this chapter, but since you'll only use them for a few of the projects, I've left them off of this list.

Photo 1 shows a typical vernier caliper; there are also versions that use dials, and some of the newer styles offer digital readouts. Whatever kind you choose, make sure it reads measurements in both metric and English dimensions.

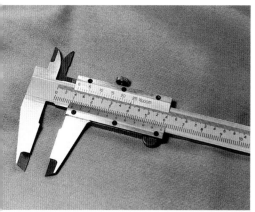

Photo 1

Annealing

The wire you purchase was formed by drawing sterling silver through a series of successively smaller holes in a drawplate until the wire reached the required diameter. This process "work hardens" the material, making it difficult to bend and shape. *Annealing*, or heating and cooling the wire again, will restore its malleability. Your supplier may carry "soft" wire that's already been annealed. If not, you can anneal the wire yourself fairly easily, and this will be the first step in any chain-making project.

Fine-gauge binding wire made from iron

You'll use this wire to hold the coiled silver wire in place during annealing. A standard-size roll seems to last forever.

Flux for annealing

The process of heating can cause metal to oxidize; on silver, this oxidation results in a black discoloration sometimes called *firescale*. Applying a coat of protective flux to the wire before heating will help prevent firescale. The flux I use for annealing wire is a mixture of three parts 99-percent alcohol and one part boracic (sometimes also called "boric") acid powder, a combination that has about the same consistency as milk. (Be sure to use the 99-percent alcohol rather than the more commonly available 66- or 70-percent varieties.) The boracic acid doesn't actually dissolve in the alcohol; instead, it's held in suspension, so you'll need to re-stir the mixture before each use.

Some books recommend a blend of sodium borate (borax) and alcohol; however, the sodium ion content in this mixture burns bright yellow when heated, making it difficult to see the dark red color of the wire as it reaches proper annealing temperature. The boracic acid/alcohol paste I use results in only the palest of green flames. You'll use a different kind of flux for soldering (page 24).

Water in a container
Paper towels
Wire cutters

Standard diagonal wire cutters work well.

A form (to coil wire around)

For wire diameters of 18 gauge (1 mm) and less, I use glass jars or other round forms such as plastic storage containers that are about 4 inches (10 cm) in diameter. Thicker wire can be too stiff to wind around such a small form, so for wires greater than 18 gauge (1 mm), I use forms ranging from 6 to 8 inches (15 to 20 cm) around.

Soft-bristle artist's paintbrush, about ⅜ inch (1 cm) across

Fireproof surface

Although you can buy proper annealing pans that are filled with pumice gravel, I find that something as simple as an old brick works just fine.

Torch and torch stand

You'll need a torch both for annealing and for soldering (page 24). Photo 2 shows the one I used to make all of the chains in this book. It's a reason-

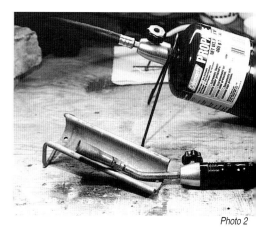

Photo 2

ably inexpensive model that uses standard propane tanks available at any hardware store. It's very similar to the units used for home plumbing, except that it has a flexible hose leading from the torch to the fuel tank. If you already own a torch of some sort, it will probably be fine for chain making.

You'll also need a small torch tip; look for one that's designated for jewelry work.

The torch stand in photo 2 is an old soldering-iron stand that I bought separately from my torch. (You should be able to find something similar wherever you purchase your torch.) A stand allows you to set the torch down without actually extinguishing the flame; this saves a lot of time, especially when you're soldering and moving from link to link.

Bamboo or copper tongs

These are used to pick up hot wire. You'll also use them when you pickle wire (see section that follows.)

How to Anneal

1 Cut four 2- to 3-inch (5 to 8 cm) lengths of the fine-gauge binding wire.

2 Coil the silver wire around the form in a tight donut shape, taking care not to leave any spaces between the strands of wire.

3 Slip the coiled wire off the form and secure it with the lengths of fine-gauge binding wire, as shown in photo 3. Be careful to "tuck in" the ends of the silver wire so they don't stick out from the body of the coil. (All of the wire needs to be heated evenly, and separate strands or loose ends can heat up more rapidly and may even melt.)

4 Use the paintbrush to completely coat both sides of the wire coil with the protective boracic-acid/alcohol-paste flux.

5 Dim the lights for this step; you'll be able to see the wire's color better. Place the coil on the fireproof surface and heat it with your torch, using a broad, hot flame until the silver glows dark red. (See the Color-Temperature Guide below.) As soon as the wire reaches this state, use your tongs to plunge the coil into the container of water. This fast cooling, or quenching, is a necessary part of the process, and the coil should not be allowed to simply air cool.

6 Use your tongs to take the coil out of the water. Remove and discard the lengths of fine-gauge binding wire, and blot the coiled wire dry with paper towels.

Photo 3

7 To remove any oxidation and residual flux, pickle the wire as described in the following section.

Pickling

Even when you use flux to protect your wire during annealing and soldering, some oxidation can occur. Additionally, the flux itself often leaves a white, powdery residue on the wire. You'll remove oxidation and flux residue by briefly soaking the wire in a hot, weak acid solution called a *pickle*.

MATERIALS & TOOLS

Pickle granules

Pickling materials for silver are generally available in the form of granules. Mixed with water, these granules form a sulfuric acid or similar solution. The manufacturer's instructions will tell you exactly how to mix your pickle.

Water in a container
Paper towels
Rubber gloves
Pickle pot

Most jewelry-supply stores carry electric pickle pots made for the purpose of keeping your pickle hot. However, an electric "crockery" slow cooker,

Color-Temperature Guide

Temperature	Color
1022°F to 1112°F (550°C to 600°C)	Very dark red
1112°F to 1202°F (600°C to 650°C)	Dark red (optimum range for silver)
1202°F to 1292°F (650°C to 700°C)	Dull cherry red
1292°F to 1382°F (700°C to 750°C)	Cherry red

such as the one shown in photo 4, makes an excellent (and usually less-expensive) substitute. Although these cookers are quite deep, you'll only

Photo 4

need a couple of inches (about 5 cm) of pickle in the bottom; otherwise, it takes too long to heat up. Pickle will also evaporate and get lost as work is dipped and removed from it. I keep track of the amount left in my pickle pot by marking a depth level on my tongs.

Bamboo or copper tongs

How to Pickle

1 You'll mix your pickle ahead of time, and use the same batch over and over. Therefore, you'll only need to perform this step when you first start chain making, or when you run low on pickle. When you have pickle already mixed, your first step will be to simply turn on the pickle pot. Don your rubber gloves; then, following the pickle manufacturer's instructions, mix the dry pickle granules with water and heat the solution in your pickle pot. (The pickle should be hot, but not boiling.)

2 Use your tongs to immerse the coil of wire (or other silver work) in the pickle; then put the cover on the pickle pot.

3 If the pickle is very hot, it may be able to clean the wire in as little as five seconds. If the pickle is cooler (but still hot), it takes a little longer. Fortunately, you can peek into the pot to see if the wire is clean yet. Just don't leave your work in the pickle too

long; the acid solution can pit the wire's surface. As you gain more experience, you'll develop a better feel for how long pickling takes under various circumstances.

4 Remove the work with your tongs, and dip it in the water to rinse it off. Pat the rinsed wire dry with paper towels.

Making Links

After the annealing and pickling processes, your silver wire should be malleable, clean, and ready to be formed into links. Before you start making links, though, you'll probably want to have some idea how many will be required to produce a chain of a given length.

Unless otherwise noted, the materials and tools list that accompanies each project specifies an amount of silver wire and an approximate number of links needed to make a chain $15\frac{3}{4}$ inches (40 cm) long. Given this information—and your handy calculator—you can easily determine the number of links needed to make the same style of chain in a different length. (It's always easier to adjust a chain's length by snipping a few extra links from its ends than it is to form, sand, solder, and polish new links added after the fact. Therefore, I suggest that you always make and solder more links than you think you'll need.)

WARNING

PICKLE IS AN ACID MATERIAL AND SHOULD BE HANDLED WITH CARE. WEAR RUBBER GLOVES WHILE MIXING THE PICKLE SOLUTION, AND AVOID BREATHING IN THE DUST FROM THE DRY PICKLE GRANULES. IF ANY PICKLE SPLASHES ONTO YOUR SKIN OR CLOTHING, RINSE IT AWAY WITH COLD WATER. KEEP THE PICKLE POT COVERED, EXCEPT WHEN YOU'RE INSERTING OR REMOVING WORK. FINALLY, AVOID GETTING IRON OR OTHER FERROUS MATERIALS IN THE PICKLE; THESE MATERIALS CAN CAUSE AN ELECTROCHEMICAL REACTION THAT IMMEDIATELY COVERS THE SILVER IN A SLIGHT COATING OF COPPER. THIS COATING MUST BE REMOVED WITH FURTHER PICKLING OR SANDING.

How to Vary Length

1 Divide the number of links specified in the materials list by 15¾ inches (40 cm), or the length noted in the project. The result of this calculation is the average number of links per inch (cm).

2 Multiply the average number of links per inch (cm) by the length of chain you want to produce. You'll probably end up with a whole number and a fraction, in which case, just round up to the next whole number.

For example, the Basic Trace Chain (page 35) requires 70 links to make a 15¾-inch

(40 cm) chain. If you wanted to make the same chain with a length of 17¾ inches (45 cm), you'd perform the following calculation:

$\underline{70}$ *(links required for original chain)*

15.75 inches *(length of original chain)*

= 4.44 links/in

4.44 links/in x **17.75** in = **78.81** links, which rounds up to **79** links

If you're working in centimeters, the new chain would be 45 centimeters long, and the calculation will look like this:

$\underline{70}$ *(links required for original chain)*

40 cm *(length of original chain)*

= 1.75 links/cm

1.75 links/cm x **45** cm = **78.75**, which rounds up to **79** links

Forming and Cutting Circular Links

Many of the projects in this book are made with circular links, or start with circular links that are shaped into ovals or oblongs after the chain has been assembled and soldered. The shaping process is described on page 30.

MATERIALS & TOOLS

Sterling-silver wire

The materials and tools list for each project will specify the required amount.

Masking tape

Tumbling shot

These tiny, highly polished bits of steel, shown in photo 5 work to deburr and polish wire. In general, they're used in conjunction with a rock tumbler (page 33) to polish entire chains. However, tumbling shot is also useful for cleaning individual links—without a tumbler—as you'll see in step 9, page 22, under the instructions for forming and cutting circular links.

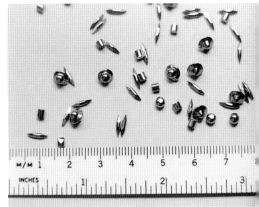

Photo 5

Be sure to thoroughly rinse and dry your tumbling shot after each use. I pour the shot into a very fine strainer, then thoroughly dry it between sheets of paper towel. When it's completely dry, I store my tumbling shot in an airtight jar until I need it again. Some people recommend that tumbling shot be stored underwater or in oil to prevent rusting; however, I've never gone to that kind of trouble, and I've been using the same batch of shot for 10 years.

Liquid dish soap

Jar of water

Mandrels

A *mandrel* is any tool that wire is coiled around to produce links. As

19

photo 6 shows, I've used all kinds of things as mandrels: everyday nails, bits of metal rod, wooden dowels, knitting needles, and many other objects with round profiles. The table to the right lists knitting needles, finishing nails, and dowels you can use as mandrels to make the projects in this book.

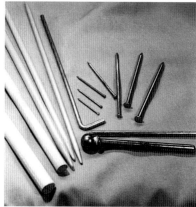

Photo 6

Diameter (mm)	(Possible) Mandrels
1.65	1 ¼-inch-long finishing nail
2	1 ½-inch-long finishing nail or No. 0 knitting needle
2.25	2-inch-long finishing nail or No. 1 knitting needle
2.5	Coat hanger wire
2.85	3-inch-long finishing nail
3.25	2 ½-inch-long common or box nail
3.5	No. 4 knitting needle
3.75	No. 5 knitting needle
4	No. 6 knitting needle
4.25	No. 7 knitting needle
5	No. 8 knitting needle
5.5	No. 9 knitting needle
6	No. 10 knitting needle
6.5	No. 10 ½ knitting needle
7	No. 10 ½ knitting needle wrapped in two layers of typing paper
8	No. 11 knitting needle
8.5	No. 11 knitting needle wrapped in two layers of typing paper
9.5	⅜-inch-diameter wooden dowel
12.5	½-inch-diameter wooden dowel

Other sizes not shown here were derived from pieces of wire such as door hinge pins found around the house. (Note: Knitting needle gauges are given by their US designation. In most other countries knitting needles are designated by their metric dimensions.)

The materials and tools list for each project only specifies mandrel size—not a specific object to be used as a mandrel—so turn back to this table for ideas about what will work. But don't just take my word for it! Be sure to use your vernier calipers to check the diameter of the actual object you choose for each mandrel.

Some of the objects suitable for use as mandrels—especially nails, steel wire, and metal-rod pieces—may have rough ends or burrs along their lengths. Use a metal file (page 26) to de-burr your mandrel before making links with it. If you're using a nail, pay special attention to the area around its point.

Bench vise

Unless you have more hands than I do, you'll need something to hold the mandrel firmly in place while you wrap the wire around it, and later, when you begin to cut, solder, and shape the links. Any heavy-duty bench vise, securely fastened to your work surface, will work.

Wire cutters

Jeweler's-saw frame and #0 blades

A *jeweler's saw* (which consists of a jeweler's-saw frame and an appropriate blade) resembles a miniature hacksaw with its blade held in place by wing nuts. Number zero (#0) piercing

blades, which are sold bundled in lots of 12, will work best for the projects in this book. When you fasten a blade in your saw frame, make sure the blade's teeth point toward the frame's handle. Secure one end of the blade in place with a wing nut; then push the frame against your workbench while you fasten the other end, as shown in photo 7. Pushing the frame against the workbench compresses the space between the saw frame's ends; when you stop pushing, the frame will "spring back" slightly, pulling the secured blade taut under tension. The blade should emit a pinging noise when you tap it with a fingernail.

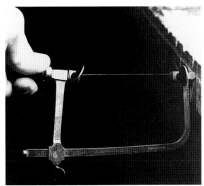

Photo 7

For someone unfamiliar with the unit, blades seem to break with frustrating regularity: Too much tension, and the blade snaps; too little, and the blade will break as you're using it. With a little practice, however, you'll be able to saw a large number of links without breaking a blade. Of course, with all that use, the blade eventually will become dull and should be discarded.

How to Make Circular Links

1 Using photo 8 a guide, place the mandrel vertically in the vise, trapping one end of the sterling-silver wire between the mandrel and the jaw of the vise.

Photo 8

2 If the mandrel is 3 millimeters or more in diameter, wind the wire around it for about 1 inch (2.5 cm). If the mandrel is smaller, wind the wire between ½ and ¾ inch (1.3 and 2 cm). Keep the spiral as tightly closed as

Photo 9

possible (photo 9). Each turn around the mandrel equals one link, so the wire size and the mandrel's diameter will determine how many links you'll get from a spiral. For instance, 16-gauge (1.25 mm) wire wound around a 4.25mm mandrel will yield about 18 links in a 1-inch (2.5 cm) spiral.

3 Snip the end of the wire and slip the spiral off of the mandrel. Trim any stubs from the ends of the spiral (photo 10).

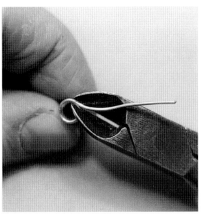

Photo 10

4. Wrap the spiral in a couple of turns of masking tape, leaving the ends open (photo 11).

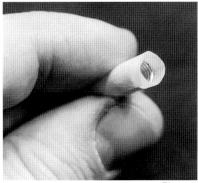

Photo 11

5 Repeat steps 1 through 4 until you have enough links for the project you're making. (Remember to always make a few more links than you think you'll need!)

6 Fix a #0 blade in one end of your jeweler's-saw frame, slip the blade through the center of one of the spirals of wire, and fasten the other end of the blade in the saw frame, as described on page 20.

7 Stand the spiral on the top of your workbench at the edge and press down on the top to hold it firmly in place. (If you don't want to cut into your workbench, use a piece of scrap board as a sawing surface.) For spirals with very small diameters, use a hacksaw to pre-cut a small slot in the surface of your workbench for the saw's blade; this will allow small-diameter spirals to sit fully on the bench without overhanging the edge. Angle the blade through the center of the spiral so that the links are cut one

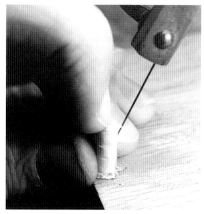

Photo 12

at a time (photo 12), rather than all at once. Don't force the saw; let it cut at its own rate.

8 Remove the masking tape from the cut spirals. There will be two partial links at each end of the spiral as a result of the cutting; discard these pieces.

9 The masking tape may leave a gummy residue on the links, and most of the links will have small burrs of metal at the cut. You can remove the masking-tape residue by pressing another piece of masking tape against each link and pulling it off again. If the links are large enough, you can smooth away the burrs with a metal file (see page 26). However, if the links are very small, or if you have large quantities of links, you can clean and de-burr them at the same time. Place them in a small jar of water along with a few drops of liquid dish soap and a heaping tablespoon of tumbling shot. Screw the jar's lid on tightly, and gently shake the whole concoction for several minutes. Rinse the clean and de-burred links with water and separate them from the tumbling shot.

Forming and Cutting Non-Circular Links

Sometimes you may want a more elliptical or rectangular shape than what can be achieved by shaping a circular link. And some chains require links that are so small that they can't even be assembled unless they're already shaped into ovals. In cases such as these, you'll need to form your links with a shaped mandrel.

The use of shaped mandrels requires a somewhat different technique from that of round mandrels. When wire is wrapped around a form, some of its springiness returns and the spiral tries to unwind a little. This isn't a problem with a circular mandrel; the links simply slip around it. But with a shaped mandrel, the spiral can't unwind the same way. It ends up gripping the mandrel, making it difficult—if not impossible—to slip off the links. To overcome this, you'll wrap the mandrel in paper before winding the wire around it. Then you'll anneal the wire while it's still on the mandrel. This will remove the wire's springiness. It will also burn off the paper, making just enough space between the mandrel and the wire to allow the links to slip off easily.

Regular-weight typing paper
Shaped mandrel
It may be difficult to find ready-made shaped mandrels in the sizes you'll need. Fortunately, many of the objects appropriate for use as round mandrels can be easily modified for use as shaped mandrels. Steps 1 through 3 below describe how to turn a 2-inch-long, finishing nail into a mandrel with a 2.25mm long axis and a 1.25mm short axis.

Hacksaw
400-grit sandpaper
You'll use sandpaper here to smooth the mandrel after you've shaped it. Later, it's also used to sand links and smooth other rough surfaces.

Materials and tools for cutting circular links (page 19)

Materials and tools for annealing (page 16)

Materials and tools for pickling (page 17)

How to Make Non-Circular Links

1 To make a shaped mandrel, start by finding an object that has a diameter that matches the long axis of the mandrel you need. For instance, a 2-inch-long finishing nail has a diameter of 2.25 mm, which is the long axis of the mandrel required to make the Tiny Oval-Link Trace Chain shown on page 43.

2 Use the hacksaw to cut off the nail's head. Clamp one end of the nail in your vise and support the underside of the other end with a block of scrap wood or with your finger (photo 13). File the top and bottom sides of the nail equally until you've reduced it to the thickness of the mandrel's required short axis. For instance, the Tiny Oval-Link Trace Chain requires a mandrel that's 1.25 mm thick along its short axis.

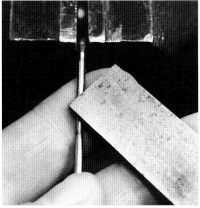

Photo 13

3 Round the mandrel's corners slightly to give it a more oval shape. Then remove the nail from the vise and use the hacksaw to cut off the stub that didn't get filed. Finish the mandrel with a light sanding.

4 Wrap the mandrel in typing paper. Larger mandrels (those that are 3 mm or more in diameter) should be wrapped in one layer of paper, with an overlap of about ¹⁄₁₆ inch (2 mm) at the edges. Secure the paper's ends with thin strips of masking tape. If you're working with a smaller mandrel, such as the one in this example, start by cutting a ¼-inch (6 mm) wide strip from the paper. Wrap this strip around the mandrel at an angle of about 45° so that each turn overlaps the previous turn by half (photo 14). The result is

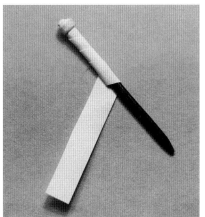

Photo 14

two layers of paper over the whole mandrel. Use thin strips of masking tape to secure the paper.

5 Clamp one end of the paper-covered mandrel in your vise. Wind the wire around the mandrel to make a tight spiral. Limit the spiral to about 12 turns; otherwise, it will be difficult to saw. A 12-turn spiral should yield about 10 usable links.

6 Remove the mandrel from the vise, strip the masking tape from the ends of the paper, and paint the spiral with flux for annealing. Place the spiral on a fireproof surface and anneal it as described on page 16. Cool the spiral in water, and slip it off the mandrel.

7 Clean and dry the mandrel before repeating steps 4 through 6 to make enough spirals to yield the required number of links.

8 Pickle all the coils (but not the mandrel) before cutting them apart, as described on page 17.

Making Jump Rings

J *ump rings* are circular links used for some purpose other than as a link in a chain. In this book, the most common use for them is as a mating ring for spring rings and other fasteners. (See chapter 7.) They can also be used to suspend pendants from chains.

Jump rings are commonly referred to by their outside dimensions, as this gives a guide to their usage. For example, a 7mm jump ring of 18-gauge (1 mm) round wire will be specified as the mating ring for a 7mm spring ring. Referring to the jump ring by its outside dimension will also help you visualize how the jump ring will relate to the size of the links in a specific chain.

MATERIALS & TOOLS

Silver wire

Mandrel
The chart on the following page lists the wire and mandrel sizes needed to make the jump rings in this book.

Vise

Jeweler's saw

Wire cutters

How to Make Jump Rings

1 To make one jump ring, start by gripping the mandrel vertically in your vise.

2 Wind a short length of wire around the mandrel for about 1½ turns.

For this Jump Ring	Use this Mandrel
4 mm of 20-gauge (0.75mm) round wire	2.5mm
5 mm of 20-gauge (0.75mm) round wire	3.5mm
5 mm of 18-gauge (1mm) round wire	3mm
6 mm of 18-gauge (1mm) round wire	4mm
6.5 mm of 16-gauge (1.25mm) round wire	4mm
7 mm of 18-gauge (1mm) round wire	5mm
7 mm of 16-gauge (1.25mm) round wire	4.5mm
7.5 mm of 16-gauge (1.25mm) round wire	5mm
8 mm of 18-gauge (1mm) round wire	6mm
9 mm of 18-gauge (1mm) round wire	7mm
9 mm of 16-gauge (1.25mm) round wire	6.5mm
9 mm of 14-gauge (1.5mm) round wire	6mm
12.5 mm of 14-gauge (1.5mm) round wire	9.5mm

3 Slip the small coil off the mandrel. It should look a lot like the spring portion of a common safety pin. (See figure 1.)

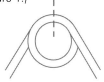

Figure 1

4 Cut the coil at the dotted line from the inside out, the same way you cut links (page 19). Note that the stubs of the wire usually aren't cut off first as they are when cutting coils of wire to make links. You can use the stubs to hold the jump ring in place while you cut it.

5 Discard the end pieces.

Sometimes, you'll simply loop a jump ring through a link and solder the jump ring closed to attach the two. Other times, you'll *butt-solder* the jump ring to another link. Butt-soldering is described in step 14 of the soldering process on page 29.

Soldering

S *oldering* is the process of joining solid metal parts (in this case, the ends of silver links) with a melted metal alloy. Many of you are probably already familiar with this process, but for those of you who aren't: Take heart! Although it takes some practice, soldering isn't hard to do.

MATERIALS & TOOLS

High-temperature solder

For making the chains in this book, the only solder you'll need is the grade specified as "easy." It's 65 percent silver, 20 percent copper, and 15 percent zinc. It begins to melt at 1240°F (671°C) and flows like water at 1325°F (718.3°C). It's usually sold in small sheets, which you'll cut into snippets before using. (Step 1 on page 27 will walk you through this process.)

Silver links

You'll need the number of links called for in the specific project you're making, plus a few spares.

Self-pickling liquid flux

This is a commercially prepared flux, specially formulated for soldering. Like the boracic acid/alcohol flux used for annealing (page 16), it will protect your work from oxidation. It will also help the solder flow more easily, and because it's slightly sticky, it will help hold the solder snippets in place on the round surface of the wire. I buy the smallest bottle available, usually about 8 ounces. You'll only use a drop or two for each soldering, so a small amount lasts a long time.

Small sable-hair artist's paintbrush
Water in a container
Envelope or small plastic bag

Either one is useful for storing solder snippets.

Metal shears

The kind I use, shown in photo 15, are called "utility grade scissors." You may also be able to find "jeweler's shears" or "minishears"—small shears specifically made for cutting thin sheet metal. You'll use these to cut the solder snippets.

Photo 15

Flat-Nose Pliers

You'll need two pairs of these pliers, both with smooth jaws that are at least ¼ inch (6 mm) across the nose. Make sure the jaws have absolutely no serrations. A jewelry-supply store is the best place to find the right kind. Don't buy the most expensive tools, though; look for a cheaper grade that hasn't been hardened to the same degree as the more costly grades. As shown in photo 16, the pliers' edges are quite sharply square, and they'll make noticeable marks on the links. To avoid this, use a flat hand file (see page 26) to sand the edges slightly smooth, as shown in photo 17. The cheaper—and softer—pliers will be easier to modify.

Chain-nose pliers

While the flat-nosed pliers described above are good for working with large and average-sized links, you'll need something more precise for small links and complex linkings. I recommend chain-nose pliers. You'll need two pairs, both with smooth jaws. As with the flat-nosed pliers, round their edges slightly with a flat hand file. File the flat end to a blunt point, too. Photo 18 shows a typical pair of chain-nose pliers as they're sold. Photo 19 shows how they should look after you've filed them.

Third-hand cross-locking tweezers

Basically, this is simply a pair of cross-locking tweezers held in a stand. As the name implies, the setup can act as a "third hand" for you by holding work

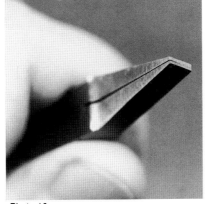

Photo 16

Photo 17

Photo 18

Photo 19

on its own. You'll also want an additional pair of cross-locking tweezers without the stand. All three pieces, shown in photo 20, are especially useful in soldering because they allow you to position a single link of a chain just over the edge of the soldering block (page 26). Thus you're able to apply heat to that one link, while the soldering block masks the other links from the torch's flame. Cross-locking tweezers usually have serrated or ribbed jaws, which is fine because they don't exert enough pressure to mark the work. If you have a choice, get tweezers with pointed ends. Most third-hand fixtures are supplied with blunt-nosed tweezers, though; just be sure to file them to a more pointed shape.

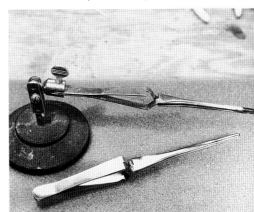

Photo 20

Fine-tip tweezers

A small pair of tweezers, with their tips filed to a point as shown in photo 21, is very useful for manipulating small links. They're also useful for turning links so that previously soldered joints are away from areas being worked on. The ones I use were originally an old pair of eyebrow tweezers.

Photo 21

Torch

I know it may seem that a special, small-flame torch would be necessary to solder such small work. However, with a little care and a soldering block (see below), you'll be able to do the job quite easily with nothing more than the same kind of torch described in the section on annealing (page 16).

Soldering block

The key to soldering small links with a relatively broad flame lies in masking the links you don't want soldered from the heat. To do this, you'll use a *soldering block*. This is basically a bar of some sort of fireproof material on which you'll solder your links. In addition to masking other links, it will protect the surface of your workbench,

and increase your torch's efficiency by reflecting heat from the torch back up to the link.

Traditional, commercially available soldering blocks are made of charcoal. You may also find blocks made from a substance called "magnesia." To me, this second type has a bit of an annoying powdery quality, but it does work well. You can even use an old house brick, although it will slowly begin to crumble with heating and cooling; however, it will be cheap and easy to replace as needed. I made many of the larger-link chains in this book with just such a brick. For smaller links, though, I recommend using a charcoal soldering block; you can cut the block to form a very sharp edge, which will allow a very small link to protrude over the edge and still mask the rest of the chain from the torch's flame.

Files and file card

You can perform the majority of the filing called for in this book with a single 6-inch (15 cm) #2-cut hand file, shown in the foreground of photo 22. The term "hand" refers to the tool's rectangular shape (not to the fact that it's used by hand), and the designation #2-cut indicates the coarseness of the file's teeth. You'll use this tool to round the edges of your pliers, to file the ends of wires, to de-burr and shape mandrels, and to remove solder bumps from and create new surfaces on links.

A few of the projects also call for needle files. These very narrow files are available in a variety of shapes, including oval, triangular (or "threesquare"),

half-round, round, and square (or "foursquare"). For the projects in this book, you'll only need the round and square shapes; however, the most economical way to buy these files—especially if you do silver work beyond chain making—is in a needle-file set, such as the one shown in photo 22.

To clean the teeth of your files, you'll use a file card. This is the tool in the background of photo 22 that looks like a short wire brush.

Photo 22

CHAIN ASSEMBLY

THE STEPS BELOW DESCRIBE ONLY THE PROCESS OF SOLDERING AND ASSEMBLING LINKS. BECAUSE MANY CHAINS CAN BE COMPLETELY ASSEMBLED AND SOLDERED BEFORE THE LINKS NEED TO BE SHAPED, THE PROCESS OF SHAPING LINKS IS DESCRIBED IN A SEPARATE SECTION (PAGE 30). HOWEVER, SOME PROJECTS WILL REQUIRE YOU TO SHAPE THE LINKS AS YOU ASSEMBLE THEM, AND MANY REQUIRE NO FURTHER SHAPING AT ALL. THE DIRECTIONS FOR EACH PROJECT WILL SPECIFY THE EASIEST AND MOST EFFICIENT ASSEMBLY METHOD FOR THAT PARTICULAR CHAIN.

How to Solder

1 Start by cutting some of your hard solder into snippets. To do this, use your shears to cut a fringe about ¼-inch (6 mm) deep along one edge of the sheet of solder, as shown in photo 23. Each strip of fringe should be a

Photo 23

little less than ¹⁄₁₆-inch (about 1 mm) wide. (The fringes tend to curl slightly, and may need to be flattened with pliers.) Cut across the fringe as shown in photo 24, placing one finger along the shear's blade to prevent the snippets from jumping all over the place as they're cut. As a general guide, the size of the snippet should be no more than the diameter of the wire being soldered, and preferably less—especially for sub-millimeter wire sizes. Store the snippets in a plastic bag or an envelope until you're ready to use them.

2 When the links are cut from the spiral, their ends won't line up with each other (figure 2.) They are offset due to the coiling, and the saw blade

Photo 24

leaves a gap equal to its own width. Begin assembling and soldering your chain by closing the first link. To do this, grasp the link with two pairs of flat-nosed pliers. Push the ends together so that they overlap just slightly and do not spring back past each other when released. This will create a bit of tension that will hold the ends together when they're aligned.

Figure 2

3 Pull the link's ends apart just a little so they can slide past each other. Then twist the link so that the ends line up (figure 3). The slight tension resulting from the previous step will hold the ends together. Make sure that the ends actually touch and are lined up properly. (Solder won't jump gaps, but it will fill the small partial gaps in a joint that result from rough, sawn ends.)

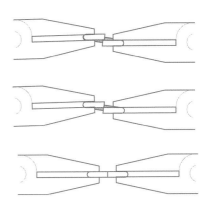

Figure 3

4 Support the closed link in one pair of your third-hand cross-locking tweezers. Place the link so that it just protrudes over the edge of your solder block (figure 4.) As you add more links, you'll drape the rest of the chain back over the body of the block.

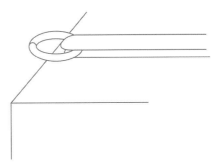

Figure 4

5 Use the sable-hair paintbrush to apply some flux over the joined ends. Then, using the damp tip of the same paintbrush, pick up a snippet of solder and place it so that it straddles the joint; this way, you'll apply flux to the solder snippet at the same time you're positioning it (figure 5).

6 Light your torch. The exact setting will depend on the size of wire you're soldering, and you'll get a feel for it with experience. Basically, the flame should be hot enough to solder the joint in five to ten seconds. If it takes too long to bring the work up to the proper temperature, the flux may burn off before the solder melts.

7 Approach the link slowly with the torch, coming at the joint from below, as shown in figure 6. (When you add more links, approaching the link from below will help mask the rest of the chain from the heat.) The idea is to dry the flux without boiling it, and a slow enough approach should allow this. (If the flux starts to boil, it can throw the solder snippet off the joint.) As the flux dries, it will leave a white, powdery substance on the link. When this appears, it means the flux has dried and you can heat the joint without disturbing the solder. Be sure to heat both sides of the joint equally, as the solder will flow to the hottest area regardless of the pull of gravity. The rectangular snippet will melt and form a ball of liquid solder; then, almost too fast for the eye to see, it will flow into the joint.

8 After the solder has flowed into the joint, remove the heat and cool the link and the tips of the tweezers holding it by plunging them into water.

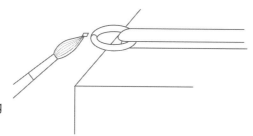

Figure 5

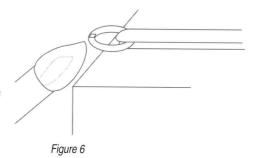

Figure 6

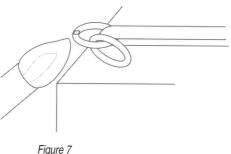

Figure 7

You can dry the link on some paper towel, but the work doesn't need to be completely dry before proceeding to the next link. If you have an appropriate torch stand, you can save time by leaving the torch lit between solderings. Just make sure the torch isn't pointing at something flammable and that you won't accidentally bump into it as you prepare the next link for soldering.

9 If the joint doesn't solder on the first try, you can usually cool it in water and try again with a small amount of additional flux and solder, unless you're working on one of the curb chains in chapter 3. Make sure that the joint is actually closed and that you apply heat where you want the solder to flow. The problem with repeated soldering, however, is that molten solder tends to dissolve the silver of the wire; this can leave a mark, or a *skull*, on your link. Skulls are hard to remove from fine wire, but they'll usually be hidden on a chain where the links overlap one another.

10 If you're working on a project that requires the links to be shaped as they're assembled, shape the soldered link as described on page 30 in the next section.

11 Twist open a second link, and slip the first one onto it. Close the unsoldered link, as described in step 3. Grip the unsoldered link in the third-hand cross-locking tweezers, and turn the soldered link so that its joint is positioned away from the joint that's about to be soldered. Place the unsoldered link so that its joint just protrudes over the edge of your soldering block. Make sure that the first link is draped back over the soldering block so that it will be masked from the torch. (See figure 7.)

12 Apply flux and a solder snippet to the unsoldered joint and heat it as described in step 7. Cool the link and the tweezers, and—if required—shape the second link. Continue to add links this way until you have a chain of the desired length.

13 After you've assembled all the links, add the fastener. (The instructions for each type of fastener will walk you through these steps.)

14 Most fasteners also require at least one jump ring. Sometimes, you'll simply loop jump rings through the necessary links and then solder the jump rings closed. On other occasions, you'll want to attach a jump ring directly to the link so that the union remains stationary. In other words, you'll want to *butt-solder* the jump ring to the link. To do this, start by soldering the jump ring closed, using the same technique described above. After you've cooled the jump ring, file

a small flat spot across its solder joint. File a similar flat spot across the link to which you'll attach the jump ring. Then position the link so that its filed spot protrudes just over the edge of your soldering block. Grasp the jump

Photo 25

ring in your third-hand cross-locking tweezers and place it against the link, flat spot to flat spot. Apply flux and a solder snippet to the joint between the two pieces, and solder them together.

15 Use the 6-inch (15 cm) #2-cut hand file to smooth any small solder bumps on the outsides of the links, and, if necessary, a round needle file to smooth the insides of the links. If you find that your links often have noticeable solder bumps in the area around the joint, you're probably using too much solder. Try using smaller snippets.

16 Pickle the chain to remove any oxidation and flux residue. (You'll pickle a soldered chain exactly the same way you pickled the annealed wire, a process described on page 17.)

WHAT IF I SOLDER LINKS TOGETHER?

SOMETIMES, IN SPITE OF ALL POSSIBLE CARE, SOME OF THE LINKS WILL GET STUCK TOGETHER DURING SOLDERING. THIS IS MOST LIKELY TO HAPPEN WHEN YOU'RE ATTEMPTING TO SOLDER SMALL LINKS CREATED FROM FINE WIRE. TO FIX THE PROBLEM, START BY GRASPING ONE OF THE STUCK LINKS WITH THE CROSS-LOCKING TWEEZERS ON THE THIRD-HAND STAND. GRASP THE OTHER STUCK LINK WITH THE FREE PAIR OF CROSS-LOCKING TWEEZERS. TRY TO WIGGLE THE LINKS APART WHILE APPLYING HEAT TO THE JOINT WITH YOUR TORCH (PHOTO 25). UNFORTUNATELY, THIS TECHNIQUE MAY CAUSE SOME ROUGHNESS ON THE SURFACE OF THE LINKS; HOWEVER, YOU CAN SMOOTH IT OUT BY APPLYING A LITTLE MORE FLUX TO THE AFFECTED AREA, MASKING THE LINKS, AND APPLYING HEAT AGAIN UNTIL THE BURRS OF ROUGH SOLDER FLOW AND DISAPPEAR. THE MELTED SOLDER MAY FORM A SLIGHT, SMOOTH BUMP ON THE LINK'S SURFACE, BUT THIS CAN BE SANDED AWAY WITH A FILE. IF REHEATING AND WIGGLING DON'T UNSTICK THE JOINT, THOUGH, ALL YOU CAN DO IS CUT OUT THE DEFECTIVE LINKS AND REPLACE THEM WITH SOME OF YOUR SPARES.

Forming "Beads"

Many of the fasteners shown in chapter 7 and several of the chain projects in this book require that you form a "bead" on the end of a piece of wire. You'll do this by melting the wire slightly to let some of the silver ball up at the end.

MATERIALS & TOOLS

Flux for annealing
Third-hand cross-locking tweezers
Torch

How to form Beads

1 Start by coating the work piece (usually a straight piece of wire, although sometimes the piece has been shaped) in annealing flux.

2 Support the work piece in your cross-locking tweezers. If it's a straight piece of wire, position it so that it's at a slight, vertical angle. (See figure 8.) If it's a link or other shaped piece, just make sure that the portion on which you want the bead is pointing down. (That way, the melted silver will ball up at the end.)

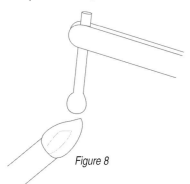

Figure 8

3 Use your torch to heat the work piece at the end on which you want the bead. Be sure to hold your torch slightly off to the side—rather than directly below the piece—while you do this. No matter how careful you are, melted silver can drop off the end of the work piece. If you're holding the torch directly under it, the silver can fall on your torch (or worse yet, your hand) and permanently damage it.

4 Heat the piece until a ball of the desired size forms. Then dip the piece in water to cool it.

Shaping Links

Most of the chains in chapters 2 and 3 are made from circular links that you'll shape into oblongs or ovals. If the links in a given chain are large enough to accommodate the mandrel around which you'll shape them and two adjacent links (see figure 9), you can assemble and solder the whole chain before shaping the links. If the links are only large enough for the mandrel and one adjacent link, you'll have to shape each link as you assemble the chain. The first method is, of course, much quicker.

Regardless of which assembly method you're using, though, the technique for shaping the links, described below, is almost identical. Figures 11a through 13a show the first method, and figures 11b through 13b show the second one. Almost all of the trace and curb chains described in this book can be made using the first method. If one requires the second, slower assembly method, the project instructions will indicate that. (Other chain styles, such as the loop-in-loop and fancy-link designs,

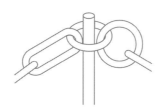

Figure 9

require different methods of shaping, and these are described within the individual projects.)

Mandrel(s)

Often, when you're working with very small circular links, you'll find that you won't be able to fit both a regular round mandrel and the adjacent link inside the link to be shaped. In these cases, you'll need to modify your mandrel slightly by filing a flat spot across half its diameter. Figure 10 shows how a modified mandrel should look, and the directions to specific projects will indicate when you need to use one.

Figure 10

Vise
Flat-nose pliers
Round-nose pliers (photo 26)

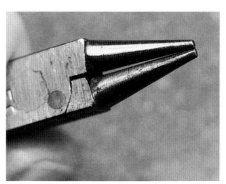

Photo 26

DRAW PLATES

THE CONVENTIONAL METHOD OF CONVERTING A CHAIN OF CIRCULAR LINKS TO OVALS OR OBLONGS IS TO DRAW THE CHAIN THROUGH A SERIES OF HOLES IN A DRAWPLATE UNTIL THE REQUIRED DIMENSION IS ACHIEVED. ALTHOUGH YOU MAY BE ABLE TO OBTAIN GREATER UNIFORMITY WITH THIS METHOD, I'VE ALWAYS BEEN QUITE PLEASED WITH THE RESULTS I GET FROM THE PROCESS DESCRIBED HERE. THUS, I'VE NEVER FOUND IT NECESSARY TO USE A DRAWPLATE, AND AM THEREFORE UNABLE TO PROVIDE ANY ADVICE ON THE USE OF ONE FOR SHAPING CHAINS. BUT IF YOU HAVE A DRAWPLATE, YOU MIGHT WANT TO GIVE IT A TRY.

How to Shape Links

1 Mount the mandrel vertically in your vise.

2 Slip a link over the mandrel, positioning it so that the solder joint will be at one end of the link (figures 11a and 11b).

3 Use one pair of your flat-nose pliers to squeeze the link around the mandrel, as shown in figures 12a and 12b.

4 Reposition the link so that the mandrel is against the unshaped end. Squeeze this end with your flat-nose pliers, as shown in figures 13a and 13b. Note that the solder joint is now

Figure 11 a

Figure 11 b

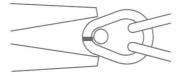

Figure 12 a

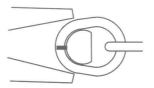

Figure 12 b

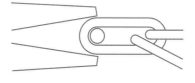

Figure 13 a

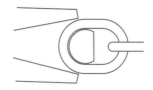

Figure 13 b

in the area where the adjacent links will overlap; this will hide the joint.

5 If you're shaping links in a chain that has already been assembled and soldered, simply repeat steps 2 through 4 until all of the links are shaped.

6 If you're shaping the links as you assemble the chain, your next step will be to twist open the next circular link, slip the shaped link onto it, and solder it closed, as described in step 11 on page 28.

Cool the link by dipping it in water. Then shape it the same way you shaped the first one. Repeat until your chain is the desired length.

7 Examine all of the links in your chain; usually, the links won't be quite flat or their sides won't be entirely straight. Use your flat-nose pliers to straighten them out as needed (photo 27).

Photo 27

Sanding the Chain

Once the chain has been soldered, pickled, and shaped, it needs a mild sanding. This is primarily to remove any marks that the pliers may have left while you were shaping the links.

400-grit and 800-grit sandpaper
The 400-grit paper will remove marks left by your tools, and the 800-grit paper will remove the fine marks that the 400-grit paper may leave. Very fine-grit papers such as these seem to be available only on waterproof backing, usually indicated by a black colored sheet. Fortunately, that waterproof backing comes in very handy here, because chains are often still wet when you sand them.

Nevertheless, you should still pat your chains dry with some paper towel before sanding.

For some chains, particularly the curb styles in chapter 3, you'll also need sanding sticks. Photo 28 shows a typical version. I make my sanding sticks by wrapping several layers of sandpaper around a piece of wood such as a paint-stirring stick. Then I secure the

Photo 28

ends with masking tape. As one layer of sandpaper wears out, simply tear it off to expose the new layer underneath.

Liquid dish soap

Nail or a short piece of wire

Vise

Two pieces of wire or strong cord, each about 3 to 4 inches (7 to 10 cm) long

Photo 29

How to Sand

1 Position the short piece of wire or nail in the vise at an angle to act as a hook.

2 Through the last link at each end of the chain, make a loop with the extra wire or the strong cord.

3 Fasten the loop at one end of the chain over the hook in the vise. Pull the rest of the chain straight with one hand. With the other hand, hold a piece of 400-grit sandpaper between your thumb and forefinger, and rub it back and forth along the length of the chain. (See photo 29.)

4 After a light sanding, loop the other end of the chain over the hook in the vise and reverse the direction of sanding. Repeat the procedure with 800-grit paper. Not much sanding is required, just enough to remove the marks from the pliers.

5 Remove the loops from the ends of the chain. Wash the chain with a few drops of liquid dish soap and some water. I simply place the chain in my palm with the soap and a little water, and rub my hands together with the chain between them. This is just a quick wash to remove grit and silver dust; however, it's important because if any grit gets into the tumbler during polishing (see the following page), it will scratch the links.

Polishing

Polishing will give your chains a bright, shiny finish. It's also a great way to restore tarnished or scratched chains to their former glory. If you're not ready to invest in a rock tumbler (the tool I use for polishing), you can give your chain its final finish with *rouge paper*. This is the material used on buffing wheels to give jewelry a mirror-like polish. It's available in a form similar to sandpaper and can give your work a tolerable finish. However, it will not polish all parts of the links, particularly the insides, the way tumble polishing does. You can also get reasonably good results from a soft toothbrush and some silver polish.

Liquid dish soap

Paper towels

Tumbling shot (See page 19 for a description.)

Small rock tumbler (photo 30)

Photo 30

How to Polish

1 Place the chain in the tumbler drum and cover it with tumbling shot to a depth of about ¾ inch (2 cm).

2 Add water to a depth of about 2 inches (5 cm); then add about 1 teaspoon of liquid dish soap.

3 Place the lid on the drum and tumble the chain for a minimum of two hours. I usually leave my chains to tumble overnight.

4 After tumbling, remove the chain, rinse it with clean water, and dry it on some paper towel. It should be bright and shiny. Be sure to rinse, dry, and properly store your tumbling shot. (See page 19 for more details.)

Finishing Touches

When the polishing is finished, you can add an appropriate fastener and, if desired, a pendant. Chapter 7 describes the processes of making several different kinds of fasteners. Several of the chains also include directions for making fasteners specific to the chain design. Of course, you're also welcome to buy a commercial fastener; just be sure to remove it first if you decide to polish the chain again. The handmade fasteners described in this book will stand up to the polishing process, but I can't vouch for fasteners that you buy; the water from the polishing process may cause the springs in them to rust.

TRACE CHAINS

Most styles of chains seem to have a variety of names. For example, the trace chains in this chapter are also sometimes called cable chains. I think part of this is due to differences between European and American designations, and part of it is probably due to advertising practices. So if you see a chain called by some name other than the one given here, we can both still be right.

There's a reason I've started the project chapters in this book with the trace (or cable) chains. These are the easiest chains to make, and if you're just learning to work with silver and to make chains, these are the ones you'll want to make first. Because these chains are geared toward beginners, I've given more attention to the basic processes of silver working here (and in the next chapter) than you'll find in later chapters. By the time you're ready to tackle the Idiot's Delight (page 62), I'll assume that you know to start by annealing your wire and to cool each link in water after you've soldered it. For the projects in this chapter, however, I've made sure to note when to do these and other basic silver-working techniques. The first project, the Basic Trace Chain on the following page, is the basis for all the chains that follow, so be sure to read through its directions before tackling any of the other projects.

⚙ *You will need 71 circular links to produce a chain that is 15 ¾ inches (40 cm) long.*

The Basic Trace Chain

THE BASIC TRACE CHAIN DETAILED HERE IS A GREAT FIRST PROJECT BECAUSE THE SIMPLE STEPS WILL FAMILIARIZE YOU WITH THE FUNDAMENTAL PROCESS OF CHAIN MAKING. AND, AS THE OTHER PROJECTS IN THIS CHAPTER DEMONSTRATE, MODEST CHANGES TO THE STEPS BELOW WILL RESULT IN CHAINS WITH QUITE DIFFERENT CHARACTERISTICS.

MATERIALS & TOOLS

- 5¼ feet (1.6 m) of 16-gauge (1.25 mm) round silver wire
- 7mm spring ring
- 7mm jump ring made from 16-gauge (1.25 mm) round silver wire
- 4.25mm round mandrel
- 2mm round mandrel

1 If you're working with hard or half-hard wire, start by annealing the wire. (See page 16.) Pickle the wire, as described on page 17; then rinse and dry it.

2 Start forming the links by winding the 16-gauge (1.25 mm) wire around the 4.25mm mandrel, as described on page 21. You'll need four 18- or 20-turn wire coils, each about 1-inch (2.5 cm) high. Remember to make a few spare links.

3 Cut the coils into links, as described on page 21.

4 Clean and de-burr the links, as described on page 22.

5 You can assemble this whole chain before soldering and shaping it. Start by closing the first link. Grasp the link in two pairs of flat-nose pliers and push its ends together so that they overlap slightly for about $1/16$ inch (1.5 mm) or so. (See figure 1.)

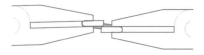

Figure 1

6 Pull the link's ends apart just a little so they can slide past each other. Then twist the link so that its ends line up, as shown in figure 2.

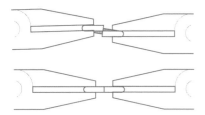

Figure 2

7 Slip a second link onto the first one. Then close the second link, as described in steps 5 and 6.

8 Continue adding links until you've assembled the entire chain.

9 Solder closed the ends of the assembled links. Start by grasping a link in your third-hand cross-locking tweezers. Place the link so that its joint just protrudes over the edge of your soldering block. Drape the rest of the chain back over the soldering block, as shown in figure 3. Apply some soldering flux to the link's joint; then place a small snippet of solder across the joint. Heat the joint from below with your torch until the solder melts and flows into the joint.

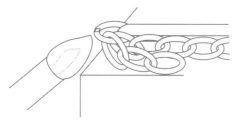

Figure 3

10 Dip the soldered link and the tips of your tweezers into some water to cool them. Then move on to the next link. Continue this way until you've soldered all the links.

11 Pickle, rinse, and dry the chain.

12 Shape the links into ovals around the 2mm mandrel. To do this, place the mandrel vertically in your vise. Slip a link over the mandrel so that the link's joint is against the mandrel and will end up at one end of the shaped link. Use your flat-nose pliers to squeeze the link around the mandrel, as shown in figure 4. Reverse the link and squeeze the other end to form an evenly shaped oval.

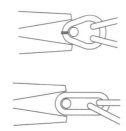

Figure 4

13 Repeat step 12 with the remaining links.

14 Butt-solder the 7mm jump ring to one end of the chain.

15 Check each link for solder bumps; file any off with your hand file. Then check to make sure the links are shaped into even ovals. Adjust them as needed with your flat-nose pliers.

16 Sand the chain using the procedure described on page 32. Remember to start with 400-grit sandpaper; then give the chain a second sanding with 800-grit paper.

17 Wash the chain with a little liquid dish soap. Then rinse it with water. Be sure that you've removed all the grit and silver sawdust in this step; if any remains on the chain, it can scratch the links during polishing.

18 Polish the chain in your tumbler for at least two hours, or until it's shiny and bright.

19 Blot the polished chain dry on some paper towel. Be sure to dry and properly store your tumbling shot, too.

20 Loop the connector ring of the spring ring through the last link on the end of the chain and twist it closed.

Another Version of the Trace Chain

SIMPLY FORMING AND SHAPING THE LINKS AROUND LARGER MANDRELS GIVES THIS TRACE CHAIN A VERY DIFFERENT LOOK FROM THE BASIC VERSION SHOWN ON PAGE 35. THE STEPS FOR MAKING THE TWO CHAINS ARE ALMOST IDENTICAL, SO I'VE ABBREVIATED THE INSTRUCTIONS SLIGHTLY FOR THIS VERSION.

MATERIALS & TOOLS

- 4½ feet (1.4 m) of 16-gauge (1.25 mm) round silver wire
- Simple Hook fastener and associated jump ring (see page 107)
- 8.5mm round mandrel
- 2.5mm round mandrel

✪ *You will need 37 circular links to produce a chain that is 15¾ inches (40 cm) long.*

1 If you're working with hard or half-hard wire, begin by annealing your wire. Then pickle and rinse it.

2 The chain in the photo is fastened with a Simple Hook fastener. You'll begin the chain's assembly with this piece, so go ahead and make it now, following the instructions on page 107.

3 Form and cut 37 links from the 16-gauge (1.25 mm) wire, using the 8.5mm mandrel as the form. Then clean and de-burr the links.

4 You can assemble this entire chain before soldering and shaping the links. Start by looping one of the links through the fat end of the hook fastener. Then, using two pairs of flat-nose pliers, close the link so that its ends overlap by about $1/16$ inch (1.5 mm). Then pull them back apart slightly and twist the link's ends together so that they press against each other and are lined up properly.

5 Loop a second link onto the first. Close this link and twist its ends into place, as described in step 4. Continue adding links until you've assembled the entire chain.

6 Solder closed the ends of the assembled links. Start by grasping a link in your third-hand cross-locking tweezers. Place it so that its joint just protrudes over the edge of your soldering block. Drape the rest of the chain back over the soldering block.

Apply some soldering flux to the link's joint; then place a small snippet of solder across the joint. Heat the link from below with your torch until the solder melts and flows into the joint.

7 Dip the soldered link into some water to cool it. Then move on to the next link. Continue this way until you've soldered closed all the links.

8 Pickle, rinse, and dry the chain.

9 Shape the links into ovals around the 2.5mm mandrel.

10 On the chain shown in the project photo, the Simple Hook fastener mates with an 8mm jump ring. Add this jump ring by butt-soldering it to the last link at the end of the chain to which the hook fastener isn't attached. Then pickle this area of the chain again to remove any discoloration.

11 Check the links for solder bumps; file any smooth with your hand file. Then use your flat-nose pliers to straighten any links that aren't evenly oval.

12 Sand the chain, starting with 400-grit sandpaper. Finish with 800-grit sandpaper. Then wash the chain thoroughly with dish detergent and water to rinse away any grit or silver sawdust.

13 Polish the chain in your tumbler.

A Trace Chain from Square Wire

S QUARE WIRE CAN ADD EXTRA SPARKLE TO A CHAIN. IT ALSO REQUIRES SLIGHTLY DIFFERENT HANDLING THAN ROUND WIRE. THE INSTRUCTIONS AND ILLUSTRATIONS BELOW WILL WALK YOU THROUGH THE DIFFERENCES; THEY'LL ALSO SHOW YOU HOW TO MAKE THIS CHAIN FOR USE WITH A PENDANT, AS IT'S PICTURED.

MATERIALS & TOOLS

- 5¾ feet (1.75 m) of 18-gauge (1 mm) square silver wire
- Toggle Clasp and associated ring (see page 108)
- 4.5mm round mandrel
- 3.5mm round mandrel with a flat spot filed on one end (see step 7)
• If you're making this chain for use with a pendant, you will also need a 9mm jump ring made from 18-gauge (1.25 mm) round wire

✿ You will need 78 circular links to produce a chain that's 15¾ inches (40 cm) long.

1 If you're working with hard or half-hard wire, anneal your wire. Then pickle and rinse it.

2 The chain shown in the photo is fastened with a Toggle Clasp. If you'd like to use this kind of fastener, make it first. (See page 108.)

3 Form the links by gripping the 4.5mm mandrel vertically in your vise, trapping one end of the square wire between the mandrel and the jaw of the vise.

4 Square wire always seems to want to twist as you wind it around the mandrel. To avoid this, use your flat-nose pliers to grip the wire close to the mandrel while you're winding it to keep the wire in the same plane. (See figure 1.) Otherwise, you'll form coils of wire, cut links from them, and clean and de-burr the links the same way you would if you were using round wire.

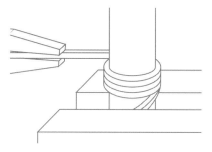

Figure 1

5 Solder and shape the links as you assemble them. Start by looping one link to the central ring of the toggle-clasp bar. Use your flat-nose pliers to close the link, overlapping the ends by about 1/16 inch (1.5 mm) to give it a bit of tension. Then twist the ends together so that they're aligned. However, because links are formed in a spiral, the ends of links made from square wire won't butt together perfectly. As long as the joint is at the end of the link where the next link will overlap it, you probably won't be able to see this slight misalignment in the final chain.

6 Grip the link in your third-hand cross-locking tweezers, and position it so that its joint protrudes just over the edge of your soldering block. Drape the toggle-clasp bar back over the block to mask it. Apply flux and a

snippet of solder to the link. Then heat it from below with your torch until the solder melts and fills the joint. Cool the link in some water and pat it dry on some paper towel.

7 A regular 3.5mm round mandrel won't fit into these links once they've been assembled as part of the chain. To make the mandrel fit, you'll need to file a flat spot on one side of it, as described on page 30.

8 Grip the modified 3.5mm mandrel in the vise. Slip the first link over it, with the round portion of the mandrel pressed against the inside of the link. Make sure that the solder joint will end up at one end of the link so that it will be hidden by the overlapping link when the chain is assembled. (See figure 2.) Use your flat-nose pliers to squeeze the link around the mandrel. Reverse the link and repeat on the other side until the link has an even, slightly oval appearance.

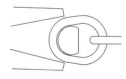

Figure 2

9 Twist open a second link and loop it onto the first link. Close and solder the ends of the second link, as described in step 6.

10 Shape the second link by slipping it over the modified 3.5mm mandrel just as you shaped the first link.

11 If you're planning to use this chain with a pendant, repeat steps 9 and 10 until you've assembled, soldered, and shaped 39 of the 78 links into a length of chain. Make a second length of chain the same way from the remaining 39 links. If you're not planning to suspend a pendant from this chain, simply assemble all 78 links into one length and skip ahead to step 13.

12 Join each of the two lengths of chain with the 9mm jump ring from which the pendant will be suspended and solder it closed. When the chain is completely finished (i.e., sanded and polished), you can add the pendant of your choice to it.

13 Attach the ring portion of the toggle clasp to the last link at the end of the chain by looping it through the last link. Then solder the ring closed.

14 Pickle, rinse, and dry the chain.

15 File off any solder bumps and straighten any links that aren't evenly oval.

16 Sand the chain, using the procedure described on page 32. Then wash it with a little liquid dish soap and rinse it clean with water.

17 Polish the chain in your tumbler. If you made this chain for use with a pendant, you can add it now.

Fetter-and-Three-Link Chain

THIS IS ONE OF MY FAVORITE VARIATIONS ON THE TRACE CHAIN. AS YOU CAN SEE IN THE PROJECT PHOTO, IT'S SIMPLY A COMBINATION OF OVAL AND CIRCULAR LINKS ASSEMBLED IN A REPEATING PATTERN. THE LONG OVAL LINKS ARE THE "FETTERS" DESCRIBED BY THIS CHAIN'S NAME.

◇ You will need 18 circular links with an inside diameter of 8.5 mm and 57 circular links with an inside diameter of 3.5 mm to make a chain that's 15¾ inches (40 cm) long.

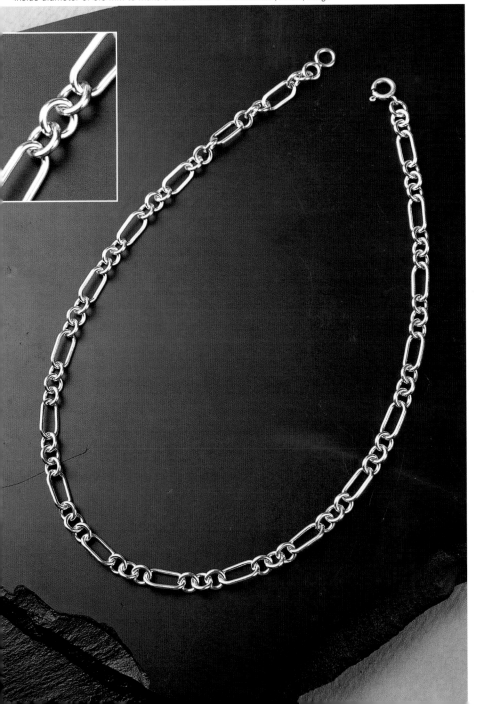

MATERIALS & TOOLS

- 5¾ feet (1.75 m) of 16-gauge (1.25mm) round silver wire
- 7mm spring ring
- 7mm jump ring made from 16-gauge (1.25 mm) round silver wire
- 8.5mm mandrel
- 3.5mm mandrel

1 If you're using wire that's hard or half-hard, start by annealing it. Then pickle, rinse, and dry the wire.

2 Form and cut 18 circular links (plus a few spares) from the 16-gauge (1.25 mm) wire, using the 8.5mm mandrel as the form.

3 Form and cut 57 circular links from the 16-gauge (1.25 mm) wire, using the 3.5mm mandrel as the form.

4 Clean and de-burr the links.

5 You can assemble the entire chain before soldering the links and shaping the large ones into ovals. Start with a small circular link. Use your flat-nose pliers to twist it closed by pushing its ends so that they overlap by about ¹⁄₁₆ inch (1.5 mm) to give the link a little tension. Then pull the ends apart slightly and align them so that they butt together.

6 Twist open another small circular link and loop it through the first one. Close the second one's ends as described in step 5. Then add a third small circular link the same way.

41

7 Now twist open a large circular link and loop it through one of the small circular links at the end of your three-link chain length. Close the large link the same way you closed the small links.

8 Add three more small circular links and another large circular link. Repeat this pattern until you've assembled all of the links. The last links at both ends of the chain should be groups of three small circular links.

9 Solder the links closed as usual.

10 Butt-solder the 7mm jump ring onto the last link at one end of the chain.

11 Pickle the soldered chain. Then rinse and dry it.

12 Shape the large links into ovals around the 3.5mm mandrel.

13 File off any solder bumps. Then examine the chain to make sure the ovals are all evenly shaped. If they're not, adjust them with your flat-nose pliers.

14 Sand the chain, using the procedure described on page 32. Then wash the chain with a little liquid dish soap, and rinse it with water.

15 Polish the chain in your tumbler.

16 Loop the connector ring of the spring ring to the end of the chain and twist it closed.

17 If you'd like to add a pendant to this chain, simply use a small jump ring to join the connector ring of your pendant through the center small circular link of the chain. This jump ring is not soldered closed.

DESIGN TIPS:

AS YOU BEGIN TO CREATE DESIGNS OF YOUR OWN, KEEP IN MIND THAT MOST TRACE CHAINS LOOK BEST IF THEY HAVE THE APPEARANCE OF A CONSISTENT WIDTH ALONG THEIR ENTIRE LENGTH. THE BASIC GUIDELINE TO REMEMBER WITH A FETTER-AND-LINK CHAIN IS THAT THE OUTSIDE DIAMETER OF THE CIRCULAR LINKS SHOULD BE THE SAME AS THE OUTSIDE WIDTH OF THE OVAL LINKS. THIS WILL GIVE THE CHAIN A CONSISTENT LOOK.

YOU CAN EASILY VARY THIS CHAIN BY ADDING A DIFFERENT NUMBER OF CIRCULAR LINKS TO THE REPEATING PATTERN. FOR INSTANCE, A FETTER-AND-FIVE-LINK CHAIN WOULD CONSIST OF AN OVAL LINK FOLLOWED BY FIVE ROUND LINKS. A FETTER-AND-ONE-LINK IS ALSO A PLEASING ARRANGEMENT. KEEP IN MIND THAT THERE SHOULD BE AN ODD NUMBER (1, 3, 5, ETC.) OF SMALL CIRCULAR LINKS IN ORDER TO KEEP THE LARGE OVAL LINKS ALL IN THE SAME PLANE.

Tiny Oval-Link Trace Chain

✱ You will need 165 oval links to make a chain that is inches (40 cm) long.

USING VERY SMALL LINKS GIVES A TRACE CHAIN A VERY POLISHED AND SOPHISTICATED APPEARANCE. HOWEVER, FORMING SUCH SMALL OVAL LINKS REQUIRES A SLIGHTLY DIFFERENT METHOD OF CONSTRUCTION AND ASSEMBLY THAN THE OTHER CHAINS IN THIS CHAPTER. THE LINKS IN THIS PROJECT ARE SO SMALL THAT THERE WOULD BE NO ROOM TO SHAPE THEM AROUND A MANDREL IF THEY WERE TO START OUT CIRCULAR. IN FACT, THE LINKS WOULDN'T EVEN FIT INTO EACH OTHER IF THEY DIDN'T START OUT AS OVALS IN THE FIRST PLACE. THIS IS AN INSTANCE WHERE YOU'LL NEED TO USE A SHAPED MANDREL TO FORM THE LINKS. BEFORE YOU GET STARTED, THOUGH, BE WARNED THAT THIS ISN'T A PROJECT FOR BEGINNING CHAIN MAKERS! (SEE THE DESIGN TIPS THAT FOLLOW THE INSTRUCTIONS.)

MATERIALS & TOOLS

- 7½ feet (2.25 m) of 18-gauge (1 mm) round silver wire
- 6mm spring ring
- 6mm jump ring made from 18-gauge (1 mm) round silver wire
- Plain typing paper
- Scissors
- 2.25mm round mandrel, modified as described in step 2
- Charcoal soldering block (optional, see step 10)

1 If you're using wire that's hard or half-hard, start by annealing it. Then pickle, rinse, and dry the wire.

2 You'll need to file your 2.25mm mandrel down until its dimensions are 1.25 millimeters by 2.25 millimeters. Be sure to review the section on Forming and Cutting Non-Circular Links on pages 22 through 23; it will walk you through the process of shaping a mandrel.

3 Cut a ¼-inch-wide (6 mm) strip from the typing paper. Wrap this around the mandrel at an angle of about 45°. Each turn should overlap the previous one by about half. (See photo 14 on page 23.) Secure the ends of the paper with small strips of masking tape.

4 Start forming the links by winding the 18-gauge (1 mm) wire around the paper-covered mandrel. Limit the coil of links to 12 or fewer turns.

5 Strip the masking tape from the ends of the paper on the mandrel. Then paint the coil with annealing flux and anneal it. Cool the coil in some water and slip it off the mandrel.

6 Clean and dry the mandrel before repeating steps 3 through 5 to form enough coils to produce the remaining links.

7 Pickle and dry the coils. Then cut them into links. (Your fingertips will probably ache, and your nails will have all kinds of notches in them by the time you finish sawing all of the coils.) Clean and de-burr the links as usual.

8 This chain must be assembled and soldered one link at a time. Start by squeezing the first link closed with your chain-nose pliers until the ends overlap slightly. Then pull the ends back and twist the link so that its ends butt against each other and are aligned properly. Hold the link in your third-hand cross-locking tweezers. Apply a little soldering flux and a small snippet of solder to its joint. Then heat the link from below with your torch. Cool the link in some water.

9 Check the link for solder bumps or burrs. If you find any on the outside of the link, file them off with your hand file. If the inside of the link needs any touch-up, use a round needle file.

10 Twist open a second link and slip it onto the first one. Twist the second link closed as before. Grasp the second link in your third-hand cross-locking tweezers, and position it over your soldering block so that its joint just protrudes over the edge. Then turn the first link so that its solder joint faces away from the second link's joint. (This will lessen the chance that you'll accidentally solder the links together.) A charcoal soldering block is best for this chain because you can carve a very sharp edge on it. Apply soldering flux and a solder snippet to the second link's joint. Then heat from below and cool as before.

11 Repeat steps 8, 9, and 10 until you've assembled and soldered all the links. As you move through the process, check to make sure you haven't soldered any links together. If this happens, all you can do is cut them out and replace them.

12 Butt-solder the 6mm jump ring to the last link at one end of the chain.

13 Pickle, rinse, and dry the chain.

14 Following the procedure described on page 32, sand the chain. Then wash it with a little soap and water.

15 Polish the chain in your tumbler.

16 Loop the connector ring of the spring ring through the last link at the end of the chain and twist it closed.

DESIGN TIPS:

THIS PROJECT REPRESENTS ABOUT THE LIMIT OF WHAT CAN BE DONE USING THE EQUIPMENT DESCRIBED IN THIS BOOK. YOU COULD MAKE SMALLER LINKS OF FINER WIRE, BUT THESE BEGIN TO NEED SPECIAL TORCHES AND TOOLS WITH VERY FINE TIPS. AS IT STANDS, THIS CHAIN WILL TEST YOUR SKILL, YOUR PATIENCE, YOUR TOOLS, AND EVEN YOUR FINGERNAILS. IT WILL PROBABLY TAKE SOME 15 OR 20 HOURS TO MAKE, AND ALTHOUGH YOU'LL BE VERY PROUD OF THE RESULTS, IT'S NOT A PROJECT WITH WHICH TO BEGIN CHAIN MAKING.

IF YOU'D LIKE A CHAIN OF THIS STYLE, BUT FEEL YOU NEED SOME EXPERIENCE FIRST, TRY MAKING IT WITH 16-GAUGE (1.25 MM) WIRE WOUND ON A 1.5MM BY 3.25MM MANDREL. THE PROPORTIONS WILL BE THE SAME, BUT THE LINKS WILL BE SLIGHTLY LARGER AND THUS EASIER TO HANDLE.

General Guidelines for Designing Your Own Trace Chains

Trace chains can be made in many interesting variations, and are excellent for jewelry applications. You can use them as bracelets, ankle chains, pocket-watch chains, and so on. After making a few of the chains described in this chapter, you'll probably want to try some ideas of your own. Here are some basic guidelines to keep in mind as you design your own chains. You'll also find these guidelines useful for the curb chains shown in the next chapter.

Finding the Right Mandrel

If there's a certain size of oval link you'd like to make from a particular diameter of wire, you can estimate the size of the required mandrel by taking the average inside diameter of the link. Just take the inside length plus the inside width and divide by two. This will be roughly the diameter of the round mandrel needed to make these links.

Let's say you want an oval link that's 6 mm wide and 10 mm long on the outside, and you want to make it from 18-gauge (1 mm wire). The inside dimensions will be the outside dimensions less two wire diameters. In this case the inside width will be 4 mm and the inside length will be 8 mm. Adding these together gives 12 mm and dividing by two gives a mandrel diameter of 6 mm .

Of course, if you're at all like me, you'll probably skip the calculations and figure out new chain dimensions by simply trying out different mandrels!

Estimating the Number of Links Required for a Given Chain Length

Given a particular size of link, you can easily estimate how many links you'll need to produce a chain of a particular length. Take the outside diameter of the link along its long axis and subtract one wire width from it. (You have to subtract one wire width because each link overlaps approximately this much.) This gives you the effective length of each link. Then divide the length of chain you want by the effective length of the link.

Let's say you want a chain that's 15¾ inches (40 cm or 400 mm) long, made from the link in our previous example. That link is 10 mm long, and made from wire with a diameter of 1 mm. Thus the effective length of each link is 9 mm. So:

• 400 mm ÷ 9 mm per link = 45 links

Estimating the Amount of Wire You'll Need

Determining the amount of wire you'll need to make a chain of a given length is just a matter of finding the outside perimeter of your links and multiplying that by the number of links needed to make the chain. To do this, you'll use the average outside diameter of your oval and multiply this by 3.14 (pi) to get the rough length of wire in each link. The total length of wire in the chain is simply this length multiplied by the number of links.

The example links were 6 mm by 10 mm, so the average outside diameter is 6 plus 10 divided by 2, which is 8 mm. Multiplying this by 3.14 (pi) gives a total wire length of 25 mm for each link.

Since we already know that the chain will require 45 links, the total amount of wire in the chain will be 25 times 45, which is 1,125 mm, or 1.125 meters.

None of these calculations is perfectly accurate; they're really just methods for getting an initial estimate of what is required. Even with the calculations, I still make sample pieces of chain to verify what I'll actually need. (To do this, just assemble 10 or 12 links of type you plan to use and shape them as necessary.)

Consistent Width

A trace chain will generally look best if it has the appearance of a consistent width along its entire length. Perhaps the only general exception to this rule is when larger or longer links are joined by a single circular link. In this case, the larger links are all close together, and the small joining links don't really contribute to the overall appearance of width; these circular links can be just big enough to hold the two adjacent links.

How Small Can You Go?

As you've probably already noticed, there's a limit to how small a link you can make and still fit other links inside it. The inside diameter of any circular link should be no smaller than 2.25 times the diameter of the wire used. Otherwise, you'll find that assembling the chain will be almost impossible.

Chains made exclusively of oval links (that is, links you've shaped with an oval mandrel, rather than a round mandrel) can be smaller. They can have a minimum inside width of about 1.25 times the diameter of the wire, and a minimum inside length of about 2.25 times the diameter of the wire.

Sketching Your Design

If you want to find out how your design will look before making it, draw a full-size sketch of it first. This doesn't require a great deal of artistic talent, but it will give you some idea of how well your design will work. I use finely spaced graph paper so I can create fairly accurate representations of the links' dimensions. Then actually make a sample length of about 10 or 20 links; this will show you whether your design works or not, and it will allow you to check your calculations of exactly how many links will be required for the full chain.

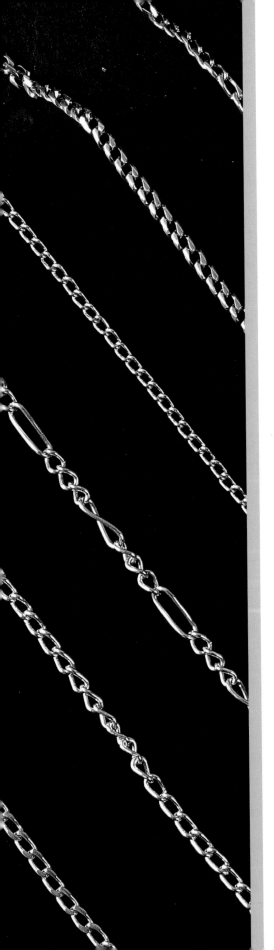

CURB CHAINS 3

I f you take a look at the trace chains described in the previous chapter, you'll notice that their links don't all lie in the same plane. When you hang a trace chain from one end, each link falls perpendicular to its immediate neighbors. And when a trace chain is strung as a necklace, its links lie in various directions on top of one another. (The chains in chapter 2 are very attractive and quite pleasing to wear, so this isn't necessarily a fault.)

The links of a curb chain, on the other hand, are twisted so that they all lie in exactly the same plane as their neighbors, and the chain as a whole lies flat. The vast majority of chains you see in jewelry stores are some form of curb chain.

The curb chains in this chapter all start out as trace chains. Then each link is twisted individually to give the chain its shape. Varying basic curb chains is almost as easy as varying basic trace chains. In addition to experimenting with different wire and mandrel sizes, the most common way to change a curb chain's appearance is to file parts of the links. The projects in this chapter will give you a good idea of the range of possibilities with curb chains. And because these chains are fairly simple to make, they're appropriate for beginners; therefore, I've continued to include some of the basic silver-working steps such as annealing wire. As in chapter 2, the first project here is the starting point for the others that follow, so its instructions are more detailed. Be sure to review the instructions for the Basic Curb Chain on the following page, even if you don't necessarily plan to make it.

○ You will need 85 links to produce a chain that is 15¾ inches (40 cm) long.

The Basic Curb Chain

ALTHOUGH THEY MIGHT NOT LOOK MUCH ALIKE, THE BASIC CURB CHAIN IS CLOSELY RELATED TO THE BASIC TRACE CHAIN SHOWN ON PAGE 35. THEY'RE ASSEMBLED, SOLDERED, AND SHAPED THE SAME WAY. HOWEVER, ALL CURB CHAINS UNDERGO ONE MORE STEP; EACH OF THEIR LINKS IS CAREFULLY TWISTED 90°. THIS TWISTING GIVES THE BASIC TRACE CHAIN A WHOLE NEW LOOK.

MATERIALS & TOOLS

- 5¾ feet (1.75 m) of 18-gauge (1 mm) round silver wire
- 6mm jump ring made of 18-gauge (1 mm) round silver wire
- 6mm spring ring
- 4mm round mandrel
- 2mm round mandrel

1 If you're working with hard or half-hard wire, start by annealing it. Then pickle and rinse the wire.

2 Form and cut 85 links (plus a few spares) from the 18-gauge (1 mm) wire, using the 4mm mandrel as the form. Clean and de-burr the links.

3 You can assemble this whole chain before soldering and shaping the links. Start by grasping the first link in two pairs of flat-nose pliers. Push the link's ends together so that they overlap slightly. Then pull the link's ends apart just a little so they can slide past each other, and twist the link so that its ends line up.

4 Slip a second link onto the first one. Then close the second link, as described in step 3.

5 Continue adding links until you've assembled the entire chain.

6 Solder closed the ends of the assembled links.

8 Earlier, I mentioned that if a link doesn't solder properly on the first try, in most cases, you can simply try again—unless you're working on a curb chain. If a link in a curb chain doesn't solder correctly, you should cut it out and replace it. Resoldering can leave additional solder on the surface of the link, causing slight malformations. While these malformations are effectively hidden in a trace chain, they're problematic for a curb chain because they affect the way it lies.

9 After you've soldered together all of the links and cut out and replaced any that didn't solder the first time, pickle and dry the chain. Then check for solder bumps and burrs; these should be filed and lightly sanded off. Be diligent—these defects can affect the lie of your chain. Don't worry if it's not perfect; small deviations won't be noticeable when the chain is worn. And the way the chain looks on the wearer's neck is the only test that really counts!

10 Shape the links into ovals around the 2mm mandrel. If any of the links come open during shaping, cut them out and replace them with new links. (Be sure to solder, pickle, and shape any new links.)

11 Check all of the links for uniformity. Use your flat-nose pliers to straighten any that aren't already properly flat ovals.

12 At this point, your chain will look very much like the Basic Trace Chain on page 35. This is the step where the two chain styles begin to diverge. Grasp each end of one of the links with flat-nose pliers. The link should be grasped so that its rounded ends are completely inside the jaws of the pliers, and only its straight sides can be seen. Be careful to center the link in the pliers. (See figure 1.)

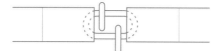

Figure 1

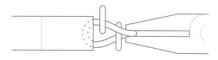

Figure 2

13 Holding the link firmly in your pliers, twist it 90°, as shown in figure 2.

14 Repeat steps 12 and 13 until you've twisted all of the links, aiming to twist each one the same amount. Try to avoid over-twisting a link, though; although you can untwist it, doing so can cause slight distortions in the piece.

15 To check your twisting of the links, suspend the chain from one end and look to see if the edges of the chain as a whole twist along its length, rather than hanging down perfectly parallel. You'll probably never get the chain to hang perfectly straight, but some deviation back and forth from perfectly straight edges is acceptable. As long as the chain doesn't twist more than 90° or so along its length, it will be fine. However, if necessary, you can go back and adjust the twist of individual links a little.

16 Once the chain is twisted to your satisfaction, check the length and adjust it as necessary by adding links or by cutting out extra links.

17 Butt-solder the jump ring that will mate with the spring ring to the last link at one end of the chain. Figure 3 shows how the pieces should look from three perspectives.

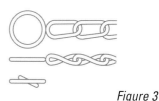

Figure 3

18 Pickle, rinse, and dry the chain. Then sand it according to the procedure described on page 32. Wash the chain with a little soap and water before tumble polishing it.

19 Finally, add the spring ring to the last link at the other end of the chain; loop the spring ring's connector ring through the last link and twist it closed.

✪ You will need 115 circular links to produce a chain that is 15¾ inches (40 cm) long.

Small-Link Curb Chain

THE EASIEST WAY TO CHANGE THE LOOK OF A DESIGN IS TO ALTER ITS DIMENSIONS. THIS DELIGHTFUL PROJECT IS SIMPLY A SMALLER, MORE DELICATE VERSION OF THE BASIC CURB CHAIN SHOWN ON PAGE 47. THE TWO CHAINS ARE MADE IN VERY MUCH THE SAME WAY, SO I'VE ABBREVIATED SOME OF THE DIRECTIONS. HOWEVER, DUE TO THE SMALL SIZE OF THE LINKS, YOU'LL NEED TO ASSEMBLE THIS CHAIN IN A SLIGHTLY DIFFERENT MANNER, AS DESCRIBED IN STEPS 3 AND 4 IN THE INSTRUCTIONS.

MATERIALS & TOOLS

- 5¾ feet (1.75 m) of 20-gauge (.75 mm) round silver wire
- 5mm jump ring made of 20-gauge (.75 mm) round silver wire
- 5mm spring ring
- 2.85mm round mandrel
- 1.65mm round mandrel
- Charcoal soldering block (optional, see step 5)

1 If you're working with hard or half-hard wire, start by annealing it. Then pickle and rinse the wire.

2 Form and cut 115 links (plus a few spares) from the 20-gauge (.75 mm) wire, using the 2.85mm mandrel as the form. Clean and de-burr the links.

3 You'll need to solder and shape the links as you assemble the chain. Start by twisting a link closed in the usual manner. Hold the link in your third-hand cross-locking tweezers. Apply flux and a snippet of solder to the joint, then gently heat the link from below. Cool the link in some water.

4 Shape the link into an oval around the 1.65mm mandrel.

5 Twist open a second link, loop it through the first one, and close it. Hold the second link in your third-hand cross-locking tweezers, and position it so that its joint protrudes just over the edge of your soldering block. If you have a charcoal soldering block, you'll want to use it for this project. Masking the first link (and subsequent links, as you add more) will be easier with the sharp edge you can cut into the charcoal. Drape the first link back over the soldering block to mask it. Add flux and a snippet of solder to the joint of the second link, then solder it closed by heating from below.

6 Shape the second link into an oval around the 1.65mm mandrel.

7 Continue to solder and shape links until you've assembled the entire chain. As you go along, check to make sure that the links are soldering closed properly and that they're not coming open as you shape them. Cut out any that don't solder closed or that have come open, and replace them with new links as you go along. (Replacing damaged links and shaping their replacements after the chain is already soldered would be very difficult due to the small size of the links.)

8 Check all the links for uniformity. Straighten any that aren't already perfectly flat ovals.

9 Pickle, rinse, and dry the chain. Then lightly file and sand off any solder bumps or burrs.

10 Twist each link 90°, using two pairs of flat-nose pliers. (Refer to figures 1 and 2 on page 48.) Avoid over-twisting a link, though; although you can untwist it, doing so can cause slight distortions in the piece.

11 Hold the chain by one end to check the overall twist. Adjust individual links as needed. Then adjust the chain's length by adding or cutting out links if needed.

12 Butt-solder the jump ring that will mate with the spring ring to the last link at one end of the chain. Figure 3 on page 48 shows how the pieces should look from three perspectives.

13 Pickle, rinse, and dry the chain. Sand it smooth; then wash it with a little soap and water before polishing it in your tumbler.

14 Finally, add the spring ring to the last link at the other end of the chain by looping the spring ring's connector ring through the last link and twist ring closed.

You will need 16 large circular links with an inside diameter of 8 mm and 51 small circular links with an inside diameter of 3.75 mm to produce a chain that's 15¾ inches (40 cm) long.

Fetter-and-Three-Link Curb Chain

WITH THE BASIC CURB CHAIN (PAGE 47), YOU SAW HOW TWISTING LINKS GIVES A TRACE STYLE CHAIN A WHOLE NEW LOOK. THE SAME IS TRUE WHEN YOU TURN A FETTER-AND-LINK TRACE CHAIN INTO A FETTER-AND-LINK CURB CHAIN. A SIMPLE HALF-TWIST GIVES THIS PROJECT ADDED ELEGANCE AND GRACE.

MATERIALS & TOOLS

- 5 feet (1.5 m) of 18-gauge (1 mm) round silver wire
- 6mm spring ring
- 6mm jump ring made from 18-gauge (1 mm) round silver wire
- 8mm round mandrel
- 3.75mm round mandrel
- 2.85mm round mandrel with a flat spot filed on one end (see step 6)

1 If you're working with hard or half-hard wire, start by annealing it. Then pickle and rinse the wire.

2 Form and cut 16 large circular links (plus a few spares) from the 18-gauge (1 mm) wire, using the 8mm mandrel as the form.

3 Form and cut 51 small circular links (plus a few spares) from the 18-gauge (1 mm) wire, using the 3.75mm mandrel as the form.

4 Clean and de-burr all the links.

5 You'll need to solder and shape each link as you assemble the chain. Start with a small circular link. Twist the link closed in the usual manner. Hold the link in your third-hand cross-locking tweezers while you solder its joint closed. Make sure the link soldered closed properly. If it didn't, discard it, and start with a new link.

6 To shape the small circular links, you'll need to start by filing a small flat spot on one end of your 2.85mm mandrel. (See page 30.) Shape the soldered small circular link into an oval around the modified end of the 2.85mm mandrel. If the link comes open during shaping, set it aside and start with a fresh link.

7 Twist open a second link and loop it through the shaped link. Twist the second link closed and position it so that its joint protrudes just over the edge of your soldering block. Solder the second link, heating from below

and making sure to mask the first link with your soldering block.

8 Shape the second small circular link around the 2.85mm mandrel. If the link comes open, replace it with a new one.

9 Add a third small circular link. Solder it closed and shape it.

10 Now loop a large circular link through the small circular link at one end of your three-link chain length. Solder the large link closed; then shape it into an oval around the 2.85mm mandrel.

11 Add three more small circular links and another large circular link, soldering and shaping them as you go. Repeat this pattern until you've assembled the entire chain.

12 Pickle, rinse, and dry the chain. Then file and lightly sand any solder bumps or burrs from the links.

13 Check all of the links for uniformity. Use your flat-nose pliers to straighten any that aren't already properly flat ovals.

14 Twist each link 90°, using two pairs of flat-nose pliers. (Refer to figures 1 and 2 on page 48.)

15 Hold the chain by one end to check the twist of it as a whole. Adjust any links that seem out of alignment.

16 Butt-solder the jump ring that will mate with the spring ring to the last link at one end of the chain, using figure 3 on page 48 as a guide.

17 Pickle, rinse, and dry the chain. Then sand it smooth and wash it with a little dish soap and water. Finish the chain by polishing it in your rock tumbler.

18 Finally, add the spring ring to the last link at the other end of the chain.

DESIGN TIPS:

I SUGGEST THAT YOU ALWAYS DESIGN FETTER-AND-LINK CHAINS SO THAT THEY ARE SYMMETRICAL ABOUT THE CENTER. THIS WILL ALLOW YOU TO LINK A PENDANT AT THE CENTER OF THE CHAIN. FOR INSTANCE, THE PROJECT DESCRIBED HERE HAS EIGHT LONG LINKS ON EACH SIDE OF A CENTRAL THREE-PIECE SECTION OF SMALL LINKS.

ALSO, WHILE TRACE-STYLE FETTER-AND-LINK CHAINS SHOULD ONLY HAVE ODD NUMBERS OF SHORT LINKS TO KEEP THE LONG LINKS IN THE SAME PLANE, NO SUCH RESTRICTION APPLIES TO CURB-STYLE FETTER-AND-LINK CHAINS. BECAUSE THE LINKS ARE ALL IN THE SAME PLANE ALREADY, ANY NUMBER OF SHORT LINKS CAN SEPARATE THE LONGER ONES. OTHER COMBINATIONS ARE POSSIBLE, AS WELL. FOR EXAMPLE, I'VE SEEN CURB-STYLE FETTER-AND-LINK CHAINS WITH ALTERNATING SEQUENCES OF THREE LONG LINKS AND THREE SHORT LINKS. YOU'LL PROBABLY WANT TO EXPERIMENT WITH IDEAS OF YOUR OWN, TOO.

You will need 85 circular links to produce a chain that's 15¾ inches (40 cm) long.

Two Versions of a Filed Curb Chain

FILING NEW SURFACES ONTO THE LINKS OF A
CURB CHAIN ADDS A GREAT DEAL TO THE
PROJECT'S APPEARANCE AND SPARKLE. THE CHAIN
TO THE RIGHT IN THE PROJECT PHOTO HAS HAD
FLAT SPOTS FILED ON THE TOP AND BOTTOM
SURFACE OF EACH LINK. THE OTHER CHAIN HAS
HAD THE SIDES OF ITS LINKS FILED AS WELL.

MATERIALS & TOOLS

- 5¾ feet (1.75 m) of 18-gauge (1 mm) round silver wire
- 6mm jump ring made from 18-gauge (1 mm) round silver wire
- 6mm spring ring
- Two spare pieces of 18-gauge (1 mm) round silver wire, each 2 to 2½ inches (5 to 6 cm) long
- 4mm round mandrel
- 2mm round mandrel
- 400-grit sanding stick
- 800-grit sanding stick

1 If you're working with hard or half-hard wire, start by annealing it. Then pickle and rinse the wire.

2 Form and cut 85 links (plus a few spares) from the 18-gauge (1 mm) wire, using the 4mm mandrel as the form. Clean and de-burr the links.

3 You can assemble this whole chain before soldering and shaping the links. Start by twisting the first link closed in the usual manner. Slip a second link onto the first one. Twist its ends closed. Continue adding links until you've assembled the entire chain. Then solder closed the ends of the assembled links.

4 After you've soldered all the links closed, check for any that didn't solder properly on the first try. Cut these out and replace them. Solder any replacement links closed.

5 Pickle, rinse, and dry the chain. Then lightly file and sand smooth any solder bumps or burrs.

6 Shape each link into an oval around the 2mm mandrel. Check each one to make sure none of them came open during the shaping process. If any did, cut them out and replace them. Solder, pickle, and shape any replacement links. Then use your flat-nose pliers to straighten any links that aren't properly flat ovals.

7 Twist each of the links 90°, using two pairs of flat-nose pliers. (Refer to figures 1 and 2 on page 48.)

8 Hold the chain by one end to check the overall twist. Use your flat-nose pliers to adjust individual links as needed. Then adjust the chain's length by adding or cutting out extra links.

9 To file the flat surfaces on the links, start by looping one of the spare pieces of wire through the last link at each end of the chain. These loops will allow you to file right up to the end links of the chain without the vise getting in the way. Clamp one of your mandrels (or a spare finishing nail) in your vise. Then hook one of the end loops over it. (This is similar to the setup you use to sand most chains; it's shown in photo 29 on page 32.)

10 Using one hand to hold the chain taut, position the forefinger of that same hand under the links being filed to support them. (See figure 1.) Use your 6-inch (15 cm) #2-cut hand file to file the top surface of each link.

If you don't plan to file the sides as well, then you can file almost halfway through the wire. If you are going to file the sides, only file the wire about a third of the way through. Be sure to file an equal amount off both sides of each link. When you've filed the top surface of all the links, reverse the chain end for end, and touch up any discrepancies that appear when you pull the chain taut from the other direction.

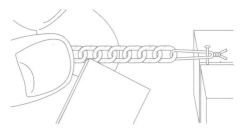

Figure 1

11 Turn the chain over and repeat step 10 on the opposite face of the chain. (I know this may sound like I'm telling you to remove half the wire from both sides, leaving nothing, but the filing on the top of the link is in a different place than the filing on the bottom.)

12 If you'd like to file the sides of the chain, reposition the mandrel or nail in the side of your vise's jaws. Rather than standing directly behind the vise (as you did to file the tops and undersides of the links), stand to the side, pulling the chain to the side as well (figure 2). Support the bottom edges of the links with one forefinger while you file the top edges with your other hand. Keep the chain pulled quite taut to prevent the links from

rolling over during the procedure. File about a third of the way through the wire. Reverse the chain end for end, and touch up any discrepancies. Then turn the chain over and file the other edge the same way.

13 Repeat the procedure on the top, bottom, and (if you're making the project to the right in the project photo) sides of the chain, this time using the 400-grit sanding stick. Repeat once again with the 800-grit sanding stick.

14 Remove the loops from the ends of the chain. Butt-solder the jump ring that will mate with the spring ring to the last link at one end of the chain. Figure 3 on page 48 shows how the pieces should look from three perspectives

15 Pickle, rinse, and dry the chain. Then sand it smooth and wash it with a little dish soap and water. Polish the chain in your rock tumbler.

16 Finally, add the spring ring to the last link at the other end of the chain.

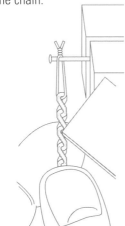

Figure 2

⚙ *You'll need 44 circular links to produce a bracelet that's 7 inches (18 cm) long. (The length of the bracelet should be adjusted to fit the intended wearer's wrist, so you may need more or fewer links.)*

filed Curb Link Bracelet

Filed CURB LINKS MADE FROM MEDIUM-WEIGHT WIRE MAKE A GOOD-LOOKING BRACELET. THE LINKS IN THIS ONE ARE FILED IN A SLIGHTLY DIFFERENT MANNER THAN THE CURB CHAIN ON PAGE 53 THAT HAS ITS TOP AND BOTTOM SURFACES FILED.

MATERIALS & TOOLS

- 3¼ feet (1 m) of 14-gauge (1.5 mm) round silver wire
- Two spare pieces of 18-gauge (1 mm) round silver wire, each 2 to 2½ inches (5 to 6 cm) long
- 7mm spring ring
- 7mm jump ring made from 18-gauge (1 mm) round silver wire
- 4mm round mandrel
- 2mm round mandrel
- 400-grit sanding stick
- 800-grit sanding stick

1 If you're working with hard or half-hard wire, start by annealing it. Then pickle and rinse the wire.

2 Form and cut 44 links (plus a few spares) from the 14-gauge (1.5 mm) wire, using the 4mm mandrel as the form. Clean and de-burr the links.

3 You'll need to solder and shape the links as you assemble the chain. Start by twisting the first link closed in the usual manner.

4 Solder the link closed. If it didn't solder properly, discard the link and start over with a new one.

5 Shape the soldered link into an oval around the 2mm mandrel. If the link comes open during shaping, discard it.

6 Open a second link, loop it through the link you just shaped, and twist it closed. Position the un-soldered link so that its joint just protrudes over the edge of your soldering block. Mask the first link by draping it back over the block. Then solder the second link closed, heating it gently from below. If the second link didn't solder properly, replace it with a fresh one.

7 Shape the second link into an oval around the 2mm mandrel. If the link comes open while you're squeezing it around the mandrel, replace it with a new link. Continue to solder and shape until you've assembled the entire bracelet.

8 Pickle, rinse, and dry the chain. Then lightly file and sand smooth any solder bumps or burrs.

9 Use your flat-nose pliers to straighten any links that aren't properly flat ovals.

10 Twist each link 90°, using two pairs of flat-nose pliers. (Refer to figures 1 and 2 on page 48.)

11 Hold the chain by one end to check the overall twist. Use your flat-nose pliers to adjust individual links as needed.

12 Adjust the chain's length by adding or cutting out links.

13 Loop one of the spare pieces of 18-gauge wire through the last link at one end of the chain; loop the other piece at the other end of the chain. Mount one of your mandrels (or a spare finishing nail) in your vise, and hook one of the end loops over it.

14 Using one hand to hold the chain taut, position the forefinger of that same hand under the links being filed to support them. (See figure 1 on page 54). Use your 6-inch (15 cm) #2-cut hand file to file about a third of the way through the wire of the link. By angling the file as you use it, you can

give the link an oval shape rather than the flat tops and sides of the previous chains. Be sure to file an equal amount off both sides of each link. When you've filed the top surface of all the links, reverse the chain end for end, and touch up any discrepancies that appear when you pull the chain taut from the other end.

15 Turn the chain over and repeat step 14 on the opposite face of the bracelet. Then repeat the procedure on each side of the chain, this time using the 400-grit sanding stick. Repeat once again with the 800-grit sanding stick.

16 Remove the wire loops from the ends of the chain. Butt-solder the jump ring that will mate with the spring ring to the last link at one end of the chain. Figure 3 on page 48 shows how the pieces should look from three perspectives.

17 Pickle, rinse, and dry the chain. Then sand it smooth and wash it with a little dish detergent and water to remove any silver sawdust or grit. Polish the chain in your rock tumbler.

18 Finally, add the spring ring to the last link at the other end of the bracelet.

filed Curb Chain from Square Wire

WHEN YOU USE SQUARE WIRE TO MAKE A FILED CURB CHAIN, THE WIRE'S "SQUARENESS" DISAPPEARS FROM THE OUTSIDE OF EACH LINK WITH FILING. HOWEVER, THE SQUARE CORNERS ARE STILL APPARENT INSIDE EACH LINK. ALTHOUGH THE EFFECT IS QUITE SUBTLE, SQUARE WIRE WILL ADD GLIMMER AND DEPTH TO ANY CHAIN.

MATERIALS & TOOLS

- 6½ feet (2 m) of 18-gauge (1 mm) square silver wire
- Two spare pieces of 18-gauge (1 mm) round silver wire, each about 2 to 2½ inches (5 to 6 cm) long
- 7mm spring ring
- 7mm jump ring made from 18-gauge (1 mm) round silver wire
- 4mm round mandrel
- 2mm round mandrel
- 400-grit sanding stick
- 800-grit sanding stick

1 If you're using hard or half-hard wire, start by annealing it. Then pickle and rinse the wire.

2 Remember that forming and cutting links from square wire requires a slightly different technique than the one used for working with round wire. To form the links, start as always, by gripping the 4mm mandrel vertically in your vise, trapping one end of the square wire between the mandrel and the jaw of the vise.

3 Square wire always seems to want to twist as you wind it around the mandrel. To avoid this, use your flat-nose pliers to grip the wire close to the mandrel while you're winding it to keep the wire in the same plane. (See figure 1 on page 40.) Cut, clean, and de-burr the links as usual.

4 You can assemble this entire chain before soldering and shaping the links. Start by twisting the first link closed in the usual manner. However, because links are formed in a spiral, the ends of links made from square wire won't butt together perfectly. As long as the joint is at the end of the link where the next link will overlap it, you won't be able to see this misalignment in the final chain. Slip a second link onto the first one and twist it closed. Continue adding links until you've assembled the entire chain.

5 Solder closed the ends of the assembled links; then check for any that didn't solder properly on the first try. Cut these out and replace them. Solder any replacement links closed.

6 Pickle, rinse, and dry the chain. Then lightly file and sand smooth any solder bumps or burrs.

7 Shape each link into an oval around the 2mm mandrel. If a link comes open during shaping, remove it, add a new link, and solder the new link closed. Then use your flat-nose pliers to straighten any links that aren't properly flat ovals.

8 Twist each link 90°, using two pairs of flat-nose pliers. (Refer to figures 1 and 2 on page 48.)

9 Hold the chain by one end to check the overall twist. Use your flat-nose pliers to adjust individual links as needed. Then adjust the chain's length by adding or cutting out links.

10 File the links. Start by filing the tops of the links, removing about a third of the wire on each one. By angling the file, you can give the chain an oval shape rather than flat tops and sides. Reverse the chain end for end, and touch up any discrepancies that appear when you pull the chain taut from the other end.

11 Turn the chain over and repeat step 10 on the opposite face of the chain. Then repeat the procedure on the top, bottom, and sides of the chain, this time using the 400-grit sanding stick. Repeat once again with the 800-grit sanding stick. (See figure 1 on page 54)

12 Remove the wire loops from the ends of the chain. Then butt-solder the jump ring that will mate with the spring ring to the last link at one end of the chain, using figure 3 on page 48 as a guide.

13 Pickle, rinse, and dry the chain. Then sand it smooth and wash it with a little dish soap and water. Polish it in your rock tumbler.

14 Finally, add the spring ring to the last link at the other end of the chain.

☼ *You will need 100 circular links to produce a chain that is 15¾ inches (40 cm) long.*

Heavy-Link Filed Curb Bracelet

THIS HANDSOME BRACELET DEMONSTRATES ABOUT THE LIMIT TO WHICH YOU CAN TAKE THE FILING OF A CURB CHAIN. YOU'LL FILE MORE THAN HALF OF THE WIRE FROM SOME PARTS OF THE LINKS—SOMETHING YOU CAN ONLY DO WITH A VERY HEAVY GAUGE OF WIRE. THEN, IN ADDITION TO FILING THE TOPS, SIDES, AND BOTTOMS, YOU'LL ALSO FILE THE ENDS OF EACH LINK. AS YOU CAN SEE, ALL OF THIS FILING COMPLETELY TRANSFORMS THE WIRE'S ORIGINAL ROUND SHAPE.

MATERIALS & TOOLS

- 3 feet (.9 m) of 12-gauge (2 mm) round silver wire
- Two spare pieces of 18-gauge (1 mm) round silver wire, each about 2 to 2½ inches (5 to 6 cm) long
- 7mm spring ring
- 7mm jump ring made from 18-gauge (1 mm) round silver wire
- 6.5mm round mandrel
- 3mm round mandrel
- 400-grit sanding stick
- 800-grit sanding stick

◉ *You will need approximately 25 circular links to produce a chain that's 7 inches (18 cm) long. (Remember that you may need to adjust the bracelet's length to fit the intended wearer's wrist.)*

1 If you're using hard or half-hard wire, start by annealing it. Then pickle and rinse the wire.

2 Form and cut 25 links (plus a few spares) from the 12-gauge (2 mm) wire, using the 6.5mm mandrel as the form. Then clean and de-burr the links.

3 You can assemble this entire bracelet before soldering and shaping the links. Start by twisting the first link closed in the usual manner. Open a second link, loop it through the first one, and twist its ends closed. Continue to add links until you've assembled the entire chain.

4 Solder closed the ends of the assembled links. Then check for any that didn't solder properly on the first try. Cut these out and replace them. Solder any replacement links closed.

5 Pickle, rinse, and dry the chain. Then lightly file and sand smooth any solder bumps or burrs.

6 Shape each link into an oval around the 3mm mandrel. If a link comes open during shaping, remove it and add a new link. Solder the new link closed; then pickle and shape it.

7 Use your flat-nose pliers to straighten any links that aren't properly flat ovals.

8 Twist the links 90°, using two pairs of flat-nose pliers. (See figures 1 and 2 on page 48.)

9 Pull the chain through your fingers, and hold it by one end to check the overall twist. Use your flat-nose pliers to adjust individual links as needed. Then adjust the bracelet's length by adding or cutting out links as needed.

10 Start by filing about halfway through the wire on the top surface of the chain. Then reverse the chain end for end, and touch up any discrepancies that appear when you pull the chain taut from the other direction.

11 Turn the chain over and repeat step 10 on the bottom face of the chain, filing about halfway through the wire on this side. Then repeat on the chain's sides.

12 Now file the ends of each link. To do this, grasp a link between your thumb and your forefinger. Hold the link against the edge of your workbench for support while you file it. (See figure 1.) Filing each link this way will take a while, because you have to do them one at a time.

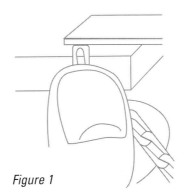

Figure 1

13 Repeat steps 10, 11, and 12, this time using the 400-grit sanding stick. Repeat once again with the 800-grit sanding stick.

14 Remove the wire loops from the ends of the chain. Then butt-solder the jump ring that will mate with the spring ring to the last link at one end of the bracelet, using figure 3 on page 48 as a guide.

15 Because of the thickness of the wire, even after it is filed, the connector of the spring ring will still not accommodate the link to which it needs to be fastened. Use your file to reduce the end of this final link to a round shape which will fit the spring ring.

16 Pickle, rinse, and dry the chain. Then sand it smooth and wash it with a little dish soap and water. Polish it in your rock tumbler.

17 Finally, add the spring ring onto the link that was filed for it in step 15.

Further Notes on Curb Chains

The Traditional Method

The traditional method of making a curb chain calls for twisting the chain as a whole, rather than one link at a time. To do this, you would fix one end of the chain in a vise and grip the other end in pliers. (You could also hold the other end by slipping a rod through the last link.) Then, you would pull the whole chain taut, and twist it by rotating the pliers (or the rod).

I'll tell you now that I've never been able to make this method work! No matter how careful I am, some links end up more twisted than others. Photo 1 shows the results of one of my attempts with the traditional method; as you can see, the links are quite inconsistently twisted. I suspect that this is probably due to differences in the annealing and soldering of the wire. For the traditional method to work, all of the links must be identical in their characteristics; otherwise, the weaker or softer links will twist more with the same amount of pressure. Professionals anneal their wire in a kiln, while amateurs like myself use a torch for this purpose; a kiln can obviously heat the wire more evenly.

Nevertheless, I wanted to find some way to make good-looking curb chains. It seemed to me that I should be able to bend the links individually. However, to make this method work, I had to figure out how much each link needed to be twisted. Did the amount of twist depend on the link's dimension? The size of the wire? The answer turned out to be very simple: No matter what size of link or thickness of wire, the twist is always 90°.

Can You Make a Curb Chain with Round Links?

Of course you can make a curb chain out of circular links. But there's a problem. Basically, the links don't seem to know which way is up, so to speak. While curb chains made with oval links tend to align themselves by their own weight, as you can see in photo 2, those made with circular links don't. They seem to take on a jumbled appearance that isn't readily self-correcting.

Almost all of the curb chains I have seen are made from oval links with inside measurement ratios, length to width, of no less than 0.8 to 1. That is, if the length of the link is taken as one unit, the width is no greater than about 80 percent of this length. For this reason, I made the small links in

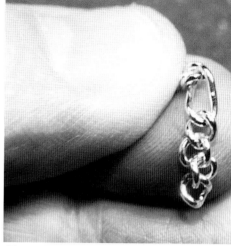

Photo 2

the Fetter-and-Three-Link Curb Chain shown on page 51 oval rather than circular.

A Final Reminder

Let me reiterate here that it pays to be ruthless in your soldering and twisting of links for curb chains. The more consistent you are, the better the result will be. On the other hand, a hobby isn't much of a hobby if it's so difficult or the standards are so high that it's no longer a pleasure. Simply do your best—your skill will increase with practice!

The quality of any curb chain depends on how carefully and consistently you twist the links. Take time to center the link in the jaws of the pliers, and make sure that the same amount is held each time. Naturally, you won't achieve machine-made perfection, but if that's what you were aiming for, you would have bought the chain in the first place. Handmade, however, is not a synonym for sloppy. The more careful you are, the better the chain will look; it will still have the minor variations that signify and beautify a handmade item.

Photo 1

THE IDIOT'S DELIGHT AND OTHER CIRCULAR LINK CHAINS 4

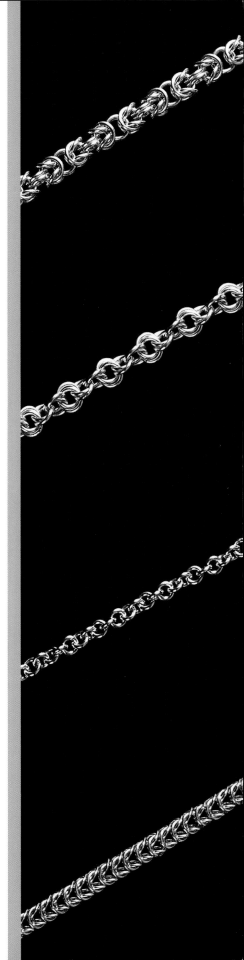

Before you try the projects in this chapter, you have to promise not to hate me for including them. I say this because I remember how I felt the first few times I tried these designs. Although assembling and soldering the Idiot's Delight (page 62) and other circular link chains isn't as difficult as it looks, learning the techniques does take time, practice, and plenty of patience. All of these chains have many small links that need to be soldered and assembled one at a time. The assembly procedures can be confusing until you get the hang of them, and the links are so tightly packed that soldering is tricky, too.

Don't be discouraged, though. Yes, these projects are time consuming and they'll test your skill to the utmost. Remember, however, that essentially you're creating future heirlooms. If you'd made an Idiot's Delight a hundred years ago and someone ran across it today, that person would admire the skill and patience of the Victorian craftsperson who had constructed it.

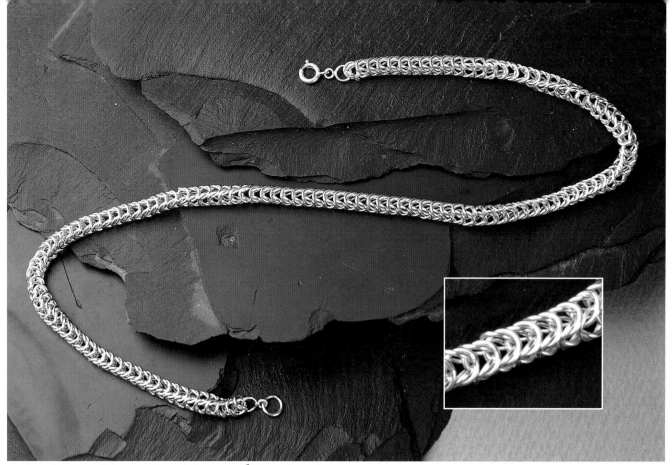

❂ *You will need 476 links to produce a chain that is 15 ¾ inches (40 cm) long.*

Idiot's Delight

I'M NOT ENTIRELY SURE HOW THIS LOVELY, SERPENTINE CHAIN GOT SUCH A TERRIBLE NAME. MAYBE IT WAS THOUGHT THAT ONLY AN IDIOT WOULD WANT TO ASSEMBLE AND SOLDER ALL OF THESE LINKS INTO A NECKLACE. YOU MAY THINK THE SAME IF YOU TRY THIS PROJECT! BEFORE YOU TRY MAKING THE IDIOT'S DELIGHT WITH SMALL SILVER LINKS, YOU MAY WANT TO PRACTICE ASSEMBLING A FEW INCHES (CM) USING A DOZEN OR SO LARGER LINKS MADE FROM COPPER WIRE. I FIND THAT LINKS MADE FROM 14-GAUGE (1.5 MM) COPPER ELECTRICAL WIRE WOUND AROUND A ³⁄₈-INCH (9.5 MM) FORM ARE EXCELLENT FOR THIS PURPOSE.

MATERIALS & TOOLS

- 20 feet (6 m) of 20-gauge (.75 mm) round silver wire
- 6mm spring ring
- 6mm jump ring made from 18-gauge (1 mm) round silver wire
- 4mm jump rings made from 20-gauge (.75 mm) round silver wire
- 3.7mm round mandrel
- Spare piece of 20-gauge (.75 mm) round silver wire, approximately 5 inches (12.5 cm) long
- Spare piece of 20-gauge (.75 mm) round silver wire, approximately 3 inches (7.5 cm) long, for use as a guide wire
- 400-grit sanding stick
- 800-grit sanding stick

1 Form and cut 476 links (plus a few spares) from the 20-gauge (.75 mm) wire, using the 3.7mm mandrel as the form. Clean and de-burr the links.

2 Start by soldering two links closed. Thread the 5-inch (12.5 cm) spare piece of silver wire through the links to tie them together. Bend this wire into a long oval and twist the ends together. This will act as a handle for holding the chain as you begin the assembly. Loop a second pair of links through the first pair, soldering each link individually as you add it. Add a third pair of links to the second, soldering each of these, too. The result should look like figure 1.

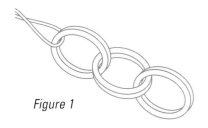

Figure 1

3 Fold back the last pair of links to either side of the central pair, as shown in figure 2.

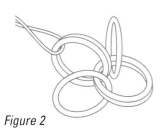

Figure 2

4 Slide the last pair (the links you folded in step 3) forward until they touch the front, inside edges of the central links, as shown in figure 3.

Figure 3

5 Using figure 4 as a reference, separate the central links and insert the guide wire through the outer links that you folded back and slid forward in steps 3 and 4. As you'll see, this forms a single, complex-looking unit of four separate loops. You will find that after you have assembled a number of these units you won't need the guide wire and can skip inserting it.

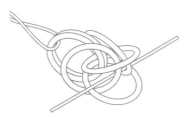

Figure 4

6 Working with one link at a time, loop a pair of new links through the folded back links, following the guide wire as shown in figure 5. (Remove the guide wire after you add the first link.)

As you add each new link in the pair, solder it closed. The best way to solder these links is to carefully position the link being soldered over your soldering block. Use your fine-tip tweezers or a piece of wire to push the other links back out of the way, making sure to turn them so that their solder joints are as far as possible from the new joint being soldered. Use a second pair of cross-locking tweezers to help mask the other links, if you find you're accidentally soldering them together. (See figure 6.) Use your smallest snippets of solder on these joints.

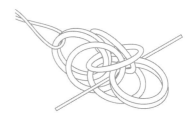

Figure 5

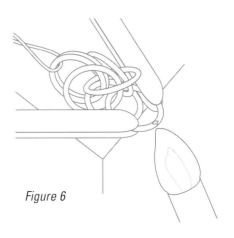

Figure 6

7 Loop another pair of links through the pair you just added, as shown in figure 7. Then repeat steps 3 through 6, starting by folding back the pair added in this step.

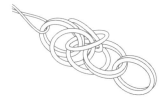

Figure 7

8 Continue to add pairs of links this way. Each time you solder a new joint, check to be sure that you haven't accidentally soldered together any links. If that happens, all you can do is cut out the affected pieces. It's almost impossible to fix this problem later, so always inspect each newly soldered joint and the surrounding links. Check for pointy solder bumps after each soldering, too. Sand them smooth with the 400-grit sanding stick. Touch up any marks with the 800-grit sanding stick. These probably won't be your best solder joints—it's very difficult to get invisible joints on such small wire. Don't worry, though; the joints are small, and after polishing, they're not very noticeable.

9 When you reach the end of the chain, stop at the step shown in figure 4. Then add another link as in figure 5, but only one link. Butt-solder a 4mm

jump ring to this final link. Then loop the 6mm jump ring through the 4mm jump ring, and solder it closed. This final jump ring will mate with the spring ring at the other end.

10 Remove the wire loop "handle" from the other end of the chain. The end of the chain should look like figure 5. Use your wire cutters to remove one of the circular loops from this end, leaving only a single link at this end of the chain. You will connect the spring ring to this link after polishing the chain. You may wonder why this link was simply not left off at the start of the chain. The reason is that if you choose to fasten the chain some other way, you may require pairs of links at each end instead of single links. For example, if you wanted to make a long circular chain in which the ends were permanently joined (and was simply slipped over the wearer's

head), you would need a pair of loops at the beginning to make this joint. The removal of a single link in this fashion is specific to modifying the chain for use with a spring-ring fastener.

11 It's not possible to evenly sand all surfaces of circular links such as these. Sanding always creates a bit of a flat or thin area on wire, and because the links in an Idiot's Delight chain can turn freely, the sanded areas won't always show in the same orientation. It's better to simply pickle and rinse the chain, then drop it directly into your tumbler with the tumbling shot. You will probably find that some pieces of tumbling shot will get caught in the links, but they should be easy to remove with your fine-tip tweezers.

12 Add the spring ring onto the end of the chain.

DESIGN TIP:

IF YOU FIND THAT THE LINKS SUGGESTED IN THIS PROJECT ARE JUST TOO SMALL TO WORK WITH, INCREASE THE SIZE OF THE MANDREL USED TO MAKE THEM BY HALF A MILLIMETER; EVEN THIS SMALL CHANGE WILL MAKE A BIG DIFFERENCE IN THE EASE OF SOLDERING.

AS A PERSONAL PREFERENCE, I WOULD SUGGEST THAT YOU USE WIRE NO LARGER THAN 20 GAUGE (.75 MM) TO MAKE THIS STYLE OF CHAIN AS A NECKLACE. OTHERWISE, IT WOULD BE TOO HEAVY. SLIGHTLY LARGER WIRE—SAY 18 GAUGE (1 MM)—DOES MAKE A NICE BRACELET, THOUGH, AS YOU'LL SEE WITH THE IDIOT'S DELIGHT BRACELET ON THE FOLLOWING PAGE. YOU MAY HOWEVER, LIKE THE LARGE, CHUNKY LOOK OF BIGGER LINKS. IF YOU DO WANT TO TRY ONE OF THESE CHAINS WITH LARGER DIAMETER WIRE, KEEP IN MIND THAT IT WILL QUICKLY GET QUITE HEAVY. THE BASIC GUIDELINE IS THAT THE MANDREL USED TO FORM THE LINKS SHOULD BE BETWEEN FOUR AND FIVE TIMES THE DIAMETER OF THE WIRE.

At first glance, you may not believe that this bracelet follows almost the same assembly procedure as the Idiot's Delight shown on page 62. Nevertheless, the projects are made almost the same way, so I've simply refered back to steps in the Idiots delight rather than repeat them here. The only difference in this bracelet is the addition of two parallel links between each four-loop "unit."

❂ *You will need 144 links to produce a bracelet that is 7½ inches (19 cm) long.*

An Idiot's Delight Bracelet

MATERIALS & TOOLS

- 10 feet (3 m) of 18-gauge (1 mm) round silver wire
- 6mm spring
- 6mm jump ring made from 18-gauge (1 mm) round silver wire
- 4mm jump ring made from 20-gauge (.75 mm) round silver wire
- Spare piece of 20-gauge (.75 mm) round silver wire, approximately 5 inches (12.5 cm) long
- Spare piece of 20-gauge (.75 mm) round silver wire, approximately 3 inches (7.5 cm) long for use as a guide wire
- 4.2mm round mandrel
- 400-grit sanding stick
- 800-grit sanding stick

1 Form and cut 144 links (plus a few spares) from the 18-gauge (1 mm) wire, using the 4.2mm mandrel as the form. Clean and de-burr the links.

2 Follow steps 2 through 7 on pages 63 through 64.

3 Loop a third pair of links through the last pair added, as shown in figure 1. Then repeat steps 2 through 7 on pages 63 through 64, starting by folding back the pair added in this step.

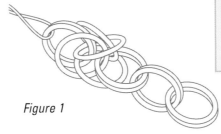

Figure 1

4 Continue to add pairs of links in the same manner. Each time you solder a new joint, check to be sure that you haven't accidentally soldered together any links. If that happens, cut out the affected pieces.

5 Finish the bracelet by following steps 9 through 12 on page 64.

DESIGN TIP:

You can vary the pattern shown in this bracelet in a number of ways. For instance, you can add the pair of parallel links after every second or third complex four-link "unit." Or you can add three pairs of parallel links between each complex link.

Wiggly Chain

This delightful, elegant chain is surprisingly easy to make. It's simply a repeating pattern of circular links looped through one another in pairs.

⚙ *You will need 210 links to produce a chain that is 15 ¾ inches (40 cm) long.*

MATERIALS & TOOLS

- About 14 feet (4.25 m) of 18-gauge (1 mm) round silver wire
- 6mm spring ring
- 6mm jump ring made from 18-gauge (1 mm) round silver wire
- 4mm jump ring made from 20-gauge (.75 mm) round silver wire
- Spare piece of 20-gauge (.75 mm) round silver wire, approximately 5 inches (12.5 cm) long
- 4.2mm round mandrel

1 Form and cut 210 links (plus a few spares) from the 18-gauge (1 mm) wire, using the 4.2mm mandrel as the form. Then clean and de-burr the links.

2 Begin by linking together two loops. Solder each link closed; then position them as shown in figure 1. Thread the 5-inch (12.5 cm) spare piece of silver wire through the links to tie them together. Bend this wire into a long oval and twist the ends together. This will act as a handle for holding the chain as you begin the assembly.

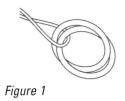

Figure 1

3 Add a third link through the links from step 2 (figure 2). Solder together the ends of the third link.

Figure 2

4 Slide the link you added in step 3 towards the center of the first two links to make some space. Then add a fourth link through all three (figure 3). Solder together the ends of this link.

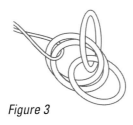

Figure 3

5 Lay the fourth link flat next to the third one. Now, repeat steps 3 and 4 to add another pair (figure 4).

Figure 4

6 Continue to add pairs of links until you only have two links left. You'll use these last two links to attach the spring-ring fastener. Loop one link only through each of the last pair of links at each end of the chain. Solder the links closed.

7 Loop the 4mm jump ring through one of the single links at one end of the chain. Then butt-solder the 4mm jump ring to the 6mm jump ring.

8 Because this chain is made from round links that will shift position constantly, it's not practical to sand it. Simply pickle and rinse it; then polish it in the tumbler.

9 Add the spring ring to the single link at the other end of the chain.

The "Simplest" Chain

I N THEORY, THERE IS NO SIMPLER CHAIN
THAN ONE MADE ENTIRELY OF CIRCULAR
LINKS. THIS MAY BE WHY SO MANY BOOKS
PRESENT IT AS AN ELEMENTARY PROJECT
FOR BEGINNERS. HOWEVER, THIS SIMPLE
CHAIN REALLY ONLY LOOKS GOOD WHEN
ITS LINKS ARE QUITE SMALL—AND
WORKING WITH SUCH TINY PIECES CAN BE
VERY CHALLENGING. YOU SHOULD HAVE
PLENTY OF EXPERIENCE WITH SOLDERING
AND BE PROFICIENT AT MASKING OTHER
LINKS BEFORE YOU TACKLE THIS PROJECT.

MATERIALS & TOOLS

- 7½ feet (2.25 m) of 18-gauge
  (1 mm) round silver wire
- 6mm spring ring
- 6mm jump ring made from 18-
  gauge (1 mm) round silver wire
- 2.65mm round mandrel
- Charcoal soldering block
  (optional)

✸ *You will need 140 links to produce a chain that is 15 ¾ inches (40 cr*

1 Form and cut 140 links (plus a few spares) from the 18-gauge (1 mm) wire, using the 2.65mm mandrel as the form. Clean and de-burr the links.

2 Because of the small size of the links, you'll need to solder each one as you assemble the chain. Start by closing the first link, just as if you were making a trace or curb chain. Hold it in your cross-locking tweezers and solder it closed as usual.

3 Twist open a second link, loop it through the first one, and twist it closed as usual.

4 If you have a charcoal soldering block, use a part which has a very sharp edge on it. If it doesn't have a suitable edge, use a sharp knife to cut a little bit off one end. If you're using an old brick as a soldering block, tap one corner with a hammer to break off a chip to produce a sharp edge.

5 Position the second link so that its joint protrudes just over the edge of your soldering block. Be very careful to turn the first link so that its joint is away from where you'll be heating. (Your fine-tip tweezers will come in handy here.) Then solder the joint, heating from below.

6 Continue to add links the same way until you've assembled the whole chain.

7 To finish the chain, butt-solder the 6mm jump ring to the last link at one end of the chain

8 Pickle, rinse, and dry the chain. This chain isn't sanded; however, if there are any noticeable marks on any of the links, touch them up with an 800-grit sanding stick.

9 Polish the chain in your tumbler.

10 Add the spring ring to the last link on the other end of the chain.

LOOP-IN-LOOP CHAINS

Like the chains in chapters 2, 3, and 4, the loop-in-loop chains form a family that differs in more ways than the use of different wire sizes. Loop-in-loop chains are interesting in that they all have a sense of volume to them. Unlike the trace and curb chains, which have distinct planes to either the individual links or to the chain as a whole, loop-in-loop projects present a distinct square or round appearance.

It's not just their appearance that differs, though. As you saw in chapter 4, the circular-link chains also have a quite different look. However, the links for loop-in-loop chains are made, shaped, and assembled in a slightly different way than the links for the other chains in this book. For that reason, the chapter is arranged in a slightly different way, too: A how-to section precedes the projects to show you how the links for these types of chains are made.

Making Links for Loop-in-Loop Chains

You'll be pleased to learn that the method for making loop-in-loop links is actually somewhat easier than the method used for other links. This style of chain tends to look better when it's made from wire that's 20 gauge (.75 mm) or less—any larger, and the resulting chain begins to look more like hardware than jewelry. When forming links with large mandrels and fine wire, it's easier to use a wooden mandrel than the typical metal objects you'd normally reach for (finishing nails, knitting needles, etc.). I use wooden dowels.

MATERIALS & TOOLS

Wooden dowel, about 8 inches (20 cm) long
(Each project's materials and tools list will give a specific diameter.)

Pencil
Drill and No. 53 or ¹⁄₁₆-in drill bit
Silver wire
(The specific projects will list the amount and dimensions.)

Two round mandrels of the same diameter
(The project instructions will give a specific diameter.)

Preparing the Dowel

1 Adjust the size of the dowel if required. (The individual project instructions will indicate if this is necessary.) From one end of the wooden dowel, measure down and mark two points, one at ¾ inch (2 cm) and one at 3½ inches (9 cm). Drill a hole through the dowel at each point using the No. 53 or ¹⁄₁₆-in drill bit.

Forming and Cutting the Links

2 Feed one end of the wire through the hole closest to the end, bend it against the dowel, and use some masking tape to hold it in place.

3 Wind the wire around the dowel by feeding the wire with one hand and turning the dowel with the other, using your thumb to maintain tension. (See photo 1.)

Photo 1

4 As you reach the number of links you want (including a few spares), cut the wire, leaving a short length to feed through the hole at 3½ inches (9 cm). While you're cutting the wire, keep the links from unwinding by maintaining pressure on them with your free hand.

5 Use a pair of flat-nose or chain-nose pliers to pull the end of wire through the hole at 3½ inches (9 cm). Pull the wire firmly to keep the links in place; then bend it down against the dowel, and wrap it and the entire coil of links in a couple of layers of masking tape.

6 Cut the links while they're still on the dowel. Start by placing the dowel against the edge of your workbench. (I've cut a small notch in the edge of mine to hold coils such as this steady while I saw.) Hold your saw at an angle between 30° and 45° to the dowel; this way, the cut will follow a slow, spiral path around the form, as shown in photo 2. As you saw, you'll usually be able to see the links spring apart slightly, indicating that you've cut through them.

Photo 2

7 When you cut through all the links, remove the masking tape and slip the links off the dowel.

8 Unfortunately, the usual method of de-burring isn't practical with this kind of link; placed in a jar or your rock tumbler with tumbling shot, the loops of wire will tend to link onto one another, forming themselves into a large ball. Instead, de-burr them by lightly passing a file over the ends of each link. File just enough to remove any roughness. (The ends won't need to butt completely flush, as the solder will fill any discrepancies in such fine wire.) Masking tape residue never seems to be a problem with this method of making links. (Perhaps the fact that the links spring apart slightly under the tape as they are cut acts to rub off any residue.)

Soldering the Links

9 To close the links, start by gently flattening the area around their ends. To do this, use flat-nose pliers to squeeze each link, as shown in photo 3. These links aren't going to remain circular, so don't worry about distorting their circular shape slightly.

Photo 3

10 Use your fingers to twist each link closed. With larger loops of fine wire such as these, you'll find that this is easier to do with your bare fingers than with pliers. As with regular links, push the ends so that they overlap just slightly to give the link a little tension to hold the ends together; then twist the ends so that they're aligned and butt together. However, don't fit the ends together with too much tension; otherwise, they'll jump out of alignment very easily.

11 You can solder the ends of each link using either of two methods. The first method is to lay the links out in groups on your soldering block or

some other fireproof surface. (See photo 4.) Apply soldering flux and a snippet of solder to each link's ends. Then solder them by moving from one to the next with your torch. The second way is to solder each link individually: Grasp a link in third-hand cross-locking tweezers and apply soldering flux and a snippet of solder to the joint. Then heat the link from below. The first way is faster, but I always found I melted more links using this method; and, for me at least, the second way tends to yield better results. Fine wire can easily overheat and melt, so regardless of which method you use, be sure to turn your flame down and approach the work slowly.

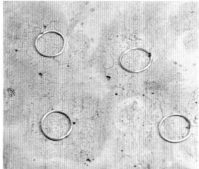

Photo 4

12 Loop all of the links together on the spare piece of silver wire. (See photo 5.) Pickle, rinse, and dry them as usual.

Photo 5

Shaping the Links into Pinched Ovals

13 Form the links into rough ovals. Start by placing a link over the ends of your round-nose pliers, making sure that the solder joint will end up at one end of the link. Gently "stretch" the link into an oval by forcing open the pliers' handles. (See photo 6 on the following page.) Make sure that you're stretching the link over a portion of the pliers that is larger than the mandrel you'll use to shape the link in the next step; otherwise, the link's ends will be too small in diameter. Repeat with the other links.

14 Form the links into proper ovals around one of the pair of smaller mandrels. (The mandrel's size will be indicated in the project instructions.) Place the mandrel in your vise and slip a link over it. Then squeeze the link into an oval with flat-nose pliers. Don't squeeze the link too much at once, though. Go back and forth a couple of times, gradually forming the oval shape; otherwise, you'll get bumps on the link's sides. Repeat with the other links. (Note that these are rather long ovals, and you'll probably need to straighten their sides and adjust them slightly to make them lie flat.)

15 Each link needs to be pinched together so that it touches at its center. To do this, start by making a jig: Place the pair of mandrels in your vise with their ends slightly angled toward each other. The mandrels should be close enough together that a link will fit over them loosely, but not so close that it will fall all the way down to the surface of the vise. Place a link over the mandrels, and pinch it in the middle with round-nose pliers. (See photo 7.) Repeat with the other links.

From this point, each of the pinched ovals is formed around another mandrel to make the actual link shape used for making the chain. However, the exact method varies from chain to chain and will be specified in each project.

Photo 6

Photo 7

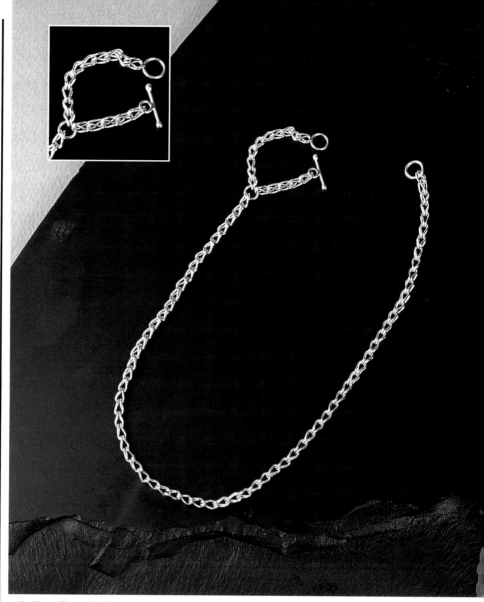

✪ *You will need 80 links to make a chain that is 15¾ inches (40 cm) long.*

Single Loop-in-Loop Chain

THIS IS THE PERFECT PROJECT TO MAKE FOR YOUR FAVORITE POCKET WATCH. A TOGGLE CLASP SUSPENDED ON A 1-INCH (2.5 CM) LENGTH OF LINKS ABOUT 2 INCHES (5 CM) FROM ONE END OF THE CHAIN MATES WITH A JUMP RING AT THAT SAME END. THIS WILL ALLOW YOU TO LOOP THE CHAIN THROUGH A BUTTONHOLE IN A JACKET OR A BLAZER. THEN ATTACH YOUR POCKET WATCH TO THE JUMP RING AT THE OTHER END OF THE CHAIN.

IF YOU WISH TO USE THIS CHAIN FOR A NECKLACE OR BRACELET, INSTRUCTIONS ARE INCLUDED FOR ADDING A SPRING-RING FASTENER IN PLACE OF THE BUTTONHOLE TOGGLE CLASP.

- 10 feet (3 m) of 20-gauge (.75 mm) round silver wire
- Wooden dowel, 3/8 inch (9.5 mm) in diameter and about 8 inches (20 cm) long
- Typing paper
- Two 2.25mm round mandrels

• **For a fastener for a chain with a pocket-watch attachment:**
  - Toggle Clasp and ring (see page 108)
  - 9mm jump ring made from 18-gauge (1 mm) round silver wire
  - 12.5mm jump ring made from 14-gauge (1.5 mm) round silver wire

• **For a fastener for a regular chain:**
  - 7mm spring ring
  - 7mm jump ring made from 18-gauge (1 mm) round silver wire
  - Two 4mm jump rings made from 20-gauge (.75 mm) round silver wire

1 Bring the wooden dowel's diameter up to $13/32$ (1 cm) by wrapping it in a couple of layers of typing paper. Hold the paper in place with a bit of masking tape at each end. Then mark and drill holes through the dowel, as described in step 1 on page 71.

2 Form and cut 80 links (plus a few spares) with the 20-gauge (.75 mm) wire, using the paper-wrapped wooden dowel as the form. (See steps 2 through 8 on page 71.)

3 Solder the ends of the links closed. (See steps 9 through 12 on page 72.)

4 Following steps 13 through 15 on page 72, shape the links into pinched ovals using the 2.25mm mandrels.

5 Mount one of the 2.25mm mandrels vertically in your vise. Use your fingers to bend a link around the mandrel. (See figure 1.) Take care to bend the link evenly so that its ends come together properly. While the link is still on the mandrel, use flat-nose pliers to squeeze it into a pear shape, as shown in figure 2.

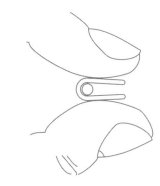

Figure 1

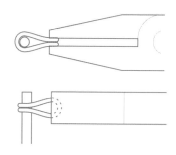

Figure 2

6 Take the link off the mandrel and turn it 90°. Slip the loops at the link's other end over the mandrel and pinch them the same way. The link should have a symmetrical appearance.

7 Repeat steps 5 and 6 to shape the rest of the links. If you're making the chain with the buttonhole fastener, continue with step 8. If you'd like to use a spring-ring fastener, skip ahead to step 14.

8 To make this project for use with a pocket watch, the chain is made in three separate pieces. Begin by slipping a link through the ring at the center of the toggle clasp bar. Grasp the link at one end with the thumb and forefinger of one hand. Insert the next link, as shown from two perspectives in figure 3.

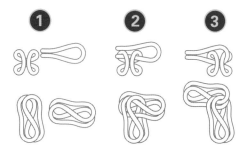

Figure 3

9 Using figure 4 (which shows the links from two perspectives) as a guide, twist the second link into proper position. The ends of the links will probably come apart slightly when you twist them into place, so pinch them back together with your flat-nose pliers The ends don't actually need to touch, but they should be consistently pinched on each link. Continue adding links until you have a 1-inch (2.5 cm) length of chain.

Figure 4

10 For the second part, butt-solder the ring portion of the toggle clasp to the end of one link. Then add additional links until you have about 2 inches (about 5 cm) of chain.

11 For the final piece, assemble a 14-inch (35.5 cm) length of chain. Then join all three pieces of chain together with the additional 9mm jump ring. Solder the jump ring closed.

12 Add the heavy 12.5mm jump ring on the end of the chain. This jump ring is not soldered closed, but is used to attach the pocket watch to the chain.

13 Pickle, rinse, and dry the chain. Skip ahead to step 18.

14 To assemble the chain for use with a spring-ring fastener, start by grasping a link at one end with the thumb and forefinger of one hand. Insert the next link, as shown in figure 3.

15 Using figure 4 as a guide, twist the second link into proper position. The ends of the links will probably come apart slightly as you twist them into position, so pinch them back together with your flat-nose pliers. The ends don't actually need to touch, but they should be consistently pinched on each link. Continue to add links until you've assembled the entire length of chain.

16 Solder closed the ends of the last link at each end of the chain. Then butt-solder a 4mm jump ring to each end link.

17 Loop a 7mm jump ring through one of the 4mm rings and solder it closed. Pickle, rinse, and dry the chain.

18 Because of the small size of the wire used in this project, sanding is not recommended. If your wire is particularly scratched, however, and requires some touch up, give the chain a light sanding with 800-grit sandpaper only. Although you'll use the usual setup for sanding this chain, don't pull too hard when you stretch it out; otherwise, you may distort the links.

19 Wash the chain with a little dish soap and water to remove any grit or silver sawdust. Then polish the chain in your tumbler. If you have made the chain for use with a spring ring fastener, you may add it on the end of the chain now.

Foxtail Chain

Y ou can see from the shape of the links how this chain gets its name—the pieces look a lot like the foxtail decorations that people used to hang from car antennae. Although this chain is made in almost the same way as the Single Loop-in-Loop Chain (page 73), a slight change in the links' proportions and shaping completely transform the Foxtail Chain's appearance.

MATERIALS & TOOLS

- 9 feet (2.75 m) of 20-gauge (.75 mm) round silver wire
- 7mm spring ring
- 7mm jump ring made from 18-gauge (1 mm) round silver wire
- Two 4mm jump rings made from 20-gauge (.75 mm) round silver wire
- Wooden dowel, ½ inch (12.5 mm) in diameter and about 8 inches (20 cm) long
- Two 2.25mm round mandrels

✺ *You will need 58 links to produce a chain that is 15 ¾ inches (40 cm) long.*

1 Mark and drill holes through the wooden dowel, as described in step 1 on page 71.

2 Form and cut 58 links (plus a few spares) with the 20-gauge (.75 mm) wire, using the ½ inch (12.5 mm) wooden dowel as the form. (See steps 2 through 8 on page 71.)

3 Solder the ends of the links closed. (See steps 9 through 12 on page 71.)

4 Following steps 13 through 15 on page 72, shape the links into pinched ovals using the 2.25mm mandrels.

5 Mount one of the 2.25mm mandrels vertically in your vise. Bend a link around it with your fingers. Take care to bend the link evenly so that its ends come together properly. Shape these links so that their sides remain straight. To do this, use your flat-nose pliers to squeeze the link around the mandrel so that its ends touch, as shown in figure 1. The ends are the only parts of the link that should touch.

6 Take the link off the mandrel and turn it 90°. Slip the loops at the link's other end over the mandrel and squeeze them the same way. The link should have a symmetrical appearance. Shape the remaining links.

7 To assemble the chain, start by grasping a link at one end with the thumb and forefinger of one hand. Insert the next link, as shown (from two perspectives) in figure 2. Using figure 3 as a guide, twist the second link into proper position. Continue adding links this way until you reach the required length.

8 To add the fastener, solder closed the ends of the last link at each end of the chain. Then butt-solder a 4mm jump ring to each end link.

9 Loop a 7mm jump ring through one of the 4mm rings and solder it closed. Pickle, rinse, and dry the chain.

10 This chain shouldn't be sanded. If your wire is very scratched, though, give it a light sanding with 800-grit sandpaper only; otherwise, you might remove too much wire. Just don't pull the chain too hard when you stretch it out to sand it; doing so may distort the links.

11 Wash the chain with a little dish soap and water to remove any grit or silver sawdust. Then polish the chain in your tumbler.

12 Attach the spring ring to the other end after the chain is polished.

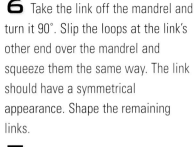

Figure 2

Figure 1

Figure 3

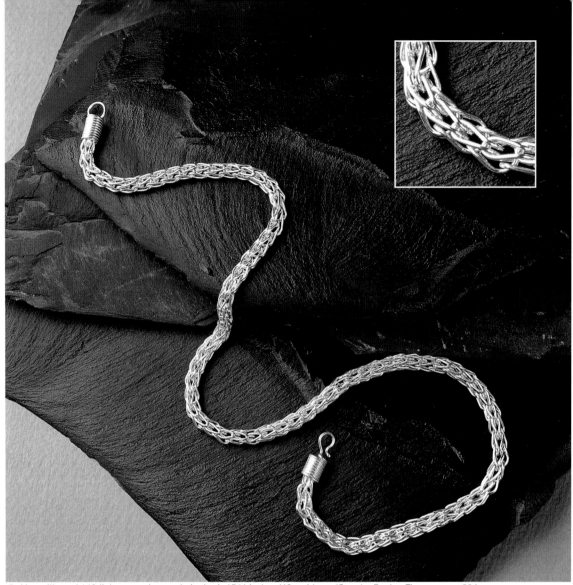

⊙ *You will need 140 links to produce a chain that's 15¾ inches (40 cm) long. (See the Design Tips on page 80.)*

Double Loop-in-Loop Chain

ALTHOUGH WE NOW KNOW THAT THIS DESIGN PREDATES THE ROMAN EMPIRE, IT'S STILL SOMETIMES CALLED A ROMAN CHAIN. IT HAS A ROUND, ROPELIKE—ALMOST WOVEN—QUALITY. THIS TEXTURE IS THE RESULT OF HOW THE CHAIN IS CONSTRUCTED; ESSENTIALLY, IT'S TWO SINGLE LOOP-IN-LOOP CHAINS (PAGE 73) "WOVEN" TOGETHER.

MATERIALS & TOOLS

- **21 feet (6.5 m) of 20-gauge (.75 mm) round silver wire**
- **End Caps with Hook and Ring Fastener (page 109)**
- **Wooden dowel, 1/2 inch (12.5 mm) in diameter and at least 8 inches (20 cm) long**
- **4mm round mandrel**
- **Two 2mm round mandrels**
- **Spare piece of 18-gauge (1 mm) round silver wire, about 2 1/2 inches (6 cm) long**
- **Silver polish**
- **Soft-bristle toothbrush**

1 Mark and drill holes through the wooden dowel, as described in step 1 on page 71.

2 Form and cut 140 links (plus a few spares) with the 20-gauge (.75 mm) wire, using the 1/2-inch (12.5 mm) wooden dowel as the form. (See steps 2 through 8 on page 71.)

3 Solder the ends of the links closed. (See steps 9 through 12 on page 72.)

4 Following steps 13 through 15 on page 72, shape the links into pinched ovals using the 2mm mandrels.

5 Mount the 4mm mandrel vertically in your vise. Bend each link into a rough horseshoe shape around the mandrel with your fingers. The links' ends shouldn't touch; and the width across the open end of each link—including the wire—should measure about 3.25 mm. (See figure 1.) Measure the first link only, and use it as a guide for forming the others.

6 Hold the 2mm mandrel in your hand, and slip the closed ends of a link over it. (See figure 2.) The mandrel will help keep the proper spacing. Then flatten the wide part of the link with your flat-nose pliers. (See figure 3.) Figure 4 shows how the shaped link should look. Shape the remaining links the same way.

7 To assemble the links, you'll need to start by making a support fixture that will maintain spacing at the start of the chain. Make this fixture by soldering the wide part of one of the links to the end of the 2 1/2-inch (6 cm) piece of wire. The link should resemble a flower on the end of a stem. (See figure 5.)

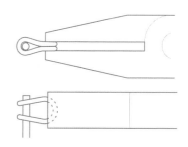

Figure 3

Figure 4

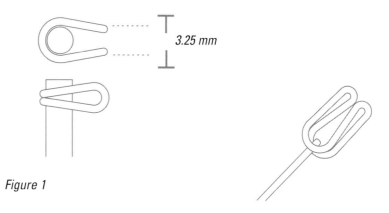

3.25 mm

Figure 1

Figure 2

Figure 5

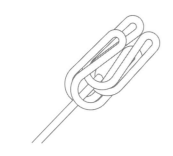

Figure 6

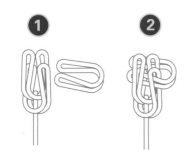

Figure 7

8 Slightly open a second link at its wide portion and slide it up the support wire until it overlaps the first link about halfway. (See figure 6.) Solder this second link to the support wire, too. To do this, lay the whole piece on your soldering block and place a couple of solder snippets where the second link touches the wire. Try to heat just that area so the two links don't get soldered together.

9 Add the next link to the chain by sliding a link through the center of the lower loops of the fixture (figure 7).

10 Insert the next link into the loop that was soldered to the end of the fixture and which is now the

second from the end of the chain. Continue adding links to the loop that is second from the end until you have only one more link to add.

11 To finish this end of the end of the chain, solder closed the last two links. Use your round-nose pliers to bring the tips of the end link together; then solder them closed. Add the last link, bring its ends together with round-nose pliers, and solder them closed as well.

12 To finish the other end (the one from which you started), remove the support fixture first. Gently heat the fixture and the links to which it's soldered until you can remove the support wire. Solder the ends of the link that was at the end of the support fixture (and is now second from the end of the chain). Then, use round-nose pliers to squeeze closed the ends of the link that is now at the end of the chain (this is the link that was

opened slightly to slide it up the support wire); solder the ends of this link closed.

13 To make the chain as it's shown on in the project photo, add the End Caps with Hook and Ring Fastener. (See page 109.)

14 Pickle the chain. Then rinse and dry it.

15 This chain is not sanded. Because of the way the links overlap and are intertwined, you simply can't reach most of the link surface. It shouldn't be polished in a tumbler, either; the tumbling shot tends to get caught in the links and is very difficult to remove. Instead, give the chain a final cleaning with commercial silver polish and a soft-bristle toothbrush. Then rinse it with warm water, using the toothbrush to remove any traces of polish.

DESIGN TIPS:

ROUND CHAINS LIKE THIS ONE TEND TO LOOK BETTER IF THEY'RE A LITTLE LONGER, SO YOU MAY WANT TO AIM FOR A LENGTH OF AT LEAST 17¾ INCHES (45 CM).

TO GIVE THIS CHAIN A REALLY GOOD POLISH, YOU CAN STRING ALL OF THE PINCHED OVALS (SEE STEP 4) TOGETHER ON SOME SPARE WIRE AND POLISH THEM IN THE TUMBLER BEFORE PROCEEDING TO STEP 5. THE LINKS AT THE ENDS OF THE CHAIN WILL LOSE SOME OF THEIR POLISH WHEN YOU ATTACH THE FASTENERS, BUT THE REST OF THE CHAIN SHOULD RETAIN MOST OF ITS BRIGHTNESS.

Triple Loop-in-Loop Chain

WEAVING TOGETHER WHAT AMOUNTS TO THREE SINGLE LOOP-IN-LOOP CHAINS (PAGE 73) GIVES THIS PROJECT A RICHLY TEXTURED, ROPELIKE QUALITY. THE TRIPLE LOOP-IN-LOOP CHAIN IS LOVELY ON ITS OWN; HOWEVER, ITS DENSE LINKINGS AND STRONG APPEARANCE MAKE THIS CHAIN PERFECT FOR USE WITH LARGE, SHOWY PENDANTS, TOO. ONE WARNING, THOUGH: THIS PROJECT REQUIRES A LOT OF WIRE!

MATERIALS & TOOLS

- 35 feet (10.5 m) of 22-gauge (.64 mm) round silver wire
- S-Hook Fastener (page 106)
- Two 6.5mm jump rings made from 16-gauge (1.25 mm) round silver wire
- Wooden dowel, ½ inch (12.5mm) in diameter and at least 8 inches (20 cm) long
- Two 1.6mm round mandrels
- 5.5mm round mandrel
- Spare piece of 20-gauge (.75mm) round silver wire, about 2½ inches (6 cm) long
- Silver polish
- Soft-bristle toothbrush

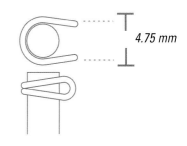

4.75 mm

Figure 1

You will need 250 links to produce a chain that is 15¾ inches (40 cm) long. (See the Design Tip on page 82.)

1 Mark and drill holes through the wooden dowel (step 1, page 71).

2 Form and cut 250 links (plus a few spares) with the 22-gauge (.64 mm) wire, using the ½-inch (12.5 mm) wooden dowel as the form (steps 2 through 8, page 71).

3 Solder the ends of the links closed (steps 9 through 12, page 72).

4 Shape the links into pinched ovals using the 1.6mm mandrels (steps 13 through 15, page 72).

5 Mount the 5.5mm mandrel vertically in your vise. Bend each link into a rough horseshoe shape around the mandrel with your fingers. The links' ends shouldn't touch, and the width across the open end of each link—including the wire—should measure 4.75 millimeters. (See figure 1.) Just measure the first link, and use it as a guide for forming the others.

6 Hold the 1.6mm mandrel in your hand, and slip the closed ends of a link over it. (See figure 2, page 79.) The mandrel will help keep the proper spacing. Flatten the wide part of the link with your flat-nose pliers. (See figure 3, page 79.) Shape the remaining links the same way.

7 To assemble the links, start by making a support fixture that will maintain spacing at the start of the chain. Make this fixture by soldering the wide part of one of the links to the end of the 2½-inch (6 cm) piece of wire. The link should resemble a flower on the end of a stem. (See figure 5 on page 79.)

8 Slightly open a second link at its wide portion. Slide a second link onto the support wire and over the first link until it overlaps the first link by two-thirds and is at an angle of about 60°. (See figure 2.) Solder it to the support wire, too.

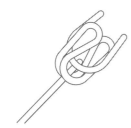

Figure 2

9 Slide a third link onto the support wire. Position the third link about halfway up the first loop and midway between the other two links as shown in figure 3. Solder this link to the support wire as well.

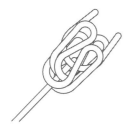

Figure 3

10 At this point you have a three-link chain soldered to the support fixture. The bottom link you just soldered onto the fixture is now the

third link from the working end of the chain. Slip the next loop through the center of this link, as shown in figure 4.

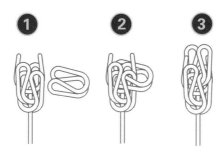

Figure 4

11 The middle link on the support fixture is now third from the working end. Slip the next loop through this link.

12 The top link on the support fixture is now third from the end. Slip the next link through it. Continue to add links to the chain, each time looping through the third-from-last link until you have only two more links to add.

13 To finish the chain's end—and to keep it from unlinking—solder closed the last three links. Use your round-nose pliers to bring the tips of the end link together; then solder them closed. Add the second-to-last link, bring its tips together with round-nose pliers, and solder them closed. Add the final link and solder it the same way. The solder joints on these last three links will be directly above each other and may touch. The three links will probably get soldered together, which is fine.

14 To finish the other end, snip off the extra wire from the support fixture. The small bit of wire left inside the chain won't be noticeable. If cutting the wire leaves a sharp edge, file it off.

15 To add an S-Hook fastener (page 106), as shown in the project photo, start by soldering closed each of the 6.5mm jump rings. File a small flat spot across the solder joints and a matching flat spot on the ends of the chain. Butt-solder the jump rings to the ends of the chain.

16 Pickle the chain. Then rinse and dry it.

17 Like the Double Loop-in-Loop Chain (page 78), this project is made of such fine wire that it shouldn't be sanded at all. I don't recommend polishing it in a tumbler, either. Instead, give the chain a final cleaning with commercial silver polish and a soft-bristle toothbrush. Then rinse it with warm water, using the toothbrush to remove any traces of polish.

DESIGN TIPS:

THIS CHAIN LOOKS BEST IF IT'S AT LEAST 17¾ INCHES (45 CM) LONG.

TO POLISH THE LINKS IN THIS CHAIN, STRING ALL OF THE PINCHED OVALS (SEE STEP 4) TOGETHER ON SOME SPARE WIRE AND POLISH THEM IN THE TUMBLER BEFORE PROCEEDING TO STEP 5.

FANCY LINK CHAINS 6

Simple trace and curb styles will probably fulfill most of your chain needs. But there are times when you need something different for a special purpose. This chapter has some suggestions for fancy link chains—projects made from links other than the simple oval and circular shapes encountered so far. As you might imagine, there are an almost infinite number of possibilities for special links, and only a few are shown here.

MATERIALS & TOOLS

– 5¾ feet (1.75 m) of 16-gauge
   (1.25mm) round silver wire
– Simple Hook fastener and
   associated ring (see page 107)
– 6.5mm round mandrel
– 2.85mm round mandrel

1 The Simple Hook fastener and its associated ring will be permanently attached to the ends of the chain, so start by making them. (The process is described on page 107.)

2 Form and cut 57 circular links (plus a few spares) from the 16-gauge (1.25 mm) wire, using the 6.5mm mandrel as the form.

3 Assemble and solder the links together, just as if you were making a Basic Trace Chain (see page 35). Be sure to slip the hook portion of the connector into the last link at one end of the chain before soldering that link closed. You'll attach the ring portion of the fastener in step 5.

✪ *You will need 57 circular links to produce a chain that is 15¾ inches (40 cm) long.*

Simple Twisted-Link Chain

ONE OF THE EASIEST WAYS TO MAKE FANCY LINKS IS TO TWIST THEM THE SAME WAY YOU'D TWIST LINKS FOR THE CURB CHAINS IN CHAPTER 3. HOWEVER, INSTEAD OF STOPPING AT 90°, CONTINUE THE TWIST FOR AT LEAST 180°. THE CHAIN SHOWN IN THE PHOTO IS ONE OF MY EARLY ATTEMPTS AT THIS STYLE OF CHAIN, AND ALTHOUGH THE RESULTING LINKS ARE NOT QUITE AS CONSISTENTLY TWISTED AS I WOULD HAVE LIKED, THE CHAIN HAS A PLEASANT HOMESPUN APPEARANCE THAT MATCHES THE ROUGH LOOK OF THE PENDANT. (I DID NOT, BY THE WAY, ACTUALLY CONSTRUCT THE PENDANT. IT STARTED LIFE AS A CAST-SILVER EARRING. WHEN ITS MATE WAS LOST, I REMOVED THE EARRING POST AND ADDED A SMALL BAIL IN ONE CORNER FROM WHICH TO SUSPEND THE EARRING.)

4 Shape the links into ovals around the 2.85mm mandrel. If you plan to add a pendant to this chain, leave the central link circular. Don't shape the fastener piece, though.

5 Butt-solder the circular ring of the hook fastener to the closed link at the end of the chain opposite the hook portion of the fastener.

6 Pickle, rinse, and dry the chain.

7 Working on one at a time, twist each link 180°. Do this by grasping each end of a link with a pair of flat-nose pliers. Give the link a half turn, making sure that you twist each link in the same direction, and that you're twisting them such that the adjacent links end up at different ends of the twisted link. (See figure 1.)

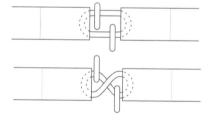

Figure 1

8 Give the chain a light sanding; then wash it with a little dish soap and rinse with water to remove any grit. Polish the chain in the tumbler.

Bow-Tie Link Chain

SMALL, SLIGHTLY OVAL RINGS JOIN LINKS WITH A SINGLE TWIST TO FORM THIS ELEGANT NECKLACE. AS IS OFTEN THE CASE WITH FANCY-LINK CHAINS, THIS ONE SUGGESTS ITS OWN FASTENER; STEPS 6 THROUGH 10 DESCRIBE THE PROCESS FOR MAKING IT.

☼ *You will need 25 large round links with an inside diameter of 9.5 mm, and 25 small round links with an inside diameter of 3.85 mm to produce a chain that is 15 ¾ inches (40 cm) long.*

- **5¼ feet (1.6 m) of 14-gauge (1.5 mm) round silver wire**
- **9mm jump ring made from 14-gauge (1.5 mm) round silver wire**
- **9.5mm round mandrel**
- **3.85mm round mandrel**
- **3.25mm round mandrel**

1 Form and cut 25 large circular links from the 14-gauge (1.5 mm) wire, using the 9.5mm mandrel as the form.

2 Form and cut 25 small circular links from the 14-gauge (1.5 mm) wire, using the 3.85mm mandrel as the form.

3 Solder together each individual large circular link. You're not assembling them yet; you're just closing their ends. Then string them together on a spare piece of silver wire, and pickle, rinse, and dry them.

4 Using the 3.25mm mandrel, shape each large circular link into an oval.

5 Working on one large link at a time, grasp each end of an oval in the jaws of your flat-nose pliers. Make sure that you have the same amount of link in the jaws of the pliers at both ends. Then, holding the pliers firmly, give the link a half-turn. (See figure 1.) Twist all the large links the same way.

6 You'll make the fastener for this chain from one of the links that you just twisted. Choose a link and start by soldering it together at its middle—

the point where it crosses over itself. This will stabilize the junction.

7 On the side of the link without the solder joint, use your jeweler's saw to cut through the link very near its center. (See figure 2.)

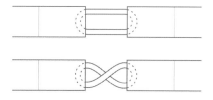

Figure 1

Figure 2

Figure 3

8 Use your round-nose pliers to open the cut end of the link. Then file off the small stub that's left at the center of the link.

9 Form a small bead on the open end of the link. (See pages 29 through 30.)

10 With your round-nose pliers, bend the open end back to its original shape; however, this time, leave a small gap between the beaded end and the rest of the link. (See figure 3.) Adjust this gap so that the final link—the 9mm jump ring—will just slip through it with a little pressure.

11 Starting with the fastener you just made, assemble the chain by alternating between twisted links and circular links. Then solder the small links closed.

12 The final link in the chain should be a small circular link; loop the 9mm jump ring through it, and solder the jump ring closed. Then pickle, rinse, and dry the chain.

13 You can leave the small links as they are, or you can squeeze them into slight ovals with your flat-nose pliers. Before you shape the links, though, turn each one so that its solder joint will be hidden by the adjoining link.

14 Give the whole chain a light sanding, paying particular attention to the fastener. Wash the chain with a little dish soap, and rinse it with water to remove any grit. Finish the chain by polishing it in your tumbler.

Double-Twisted Bow-Tie Link Chain

This chain is very similar to the Bow-Tie Link Chain shown on page 83. You'll notice that, except for the full twist in this project, the steps are almost identical for the two chains. However, the extra twist gives this necklace a slightly more intricate appearance (without a lot of intricate work!), and it shows how slight alterations can help you achieve a variety of results.

MATERIALS & TOOLS

- 4½ feet (1.4 m) of 14-gauge (1.5 mm) round silver wire
- 9mm jump ring made from 14-gauge (1.5 mm) round silver wire
- 12.5mm round mandrel
- 3.85mm round mandrel
- 3.25mm round mandrel

1 Form and cut 18 large circular links from the 14-gauge (1.5 mm) wire, using the 12.5mm mandrel as the form.

2 Form and cut 18 small circular links from the 14-gauge (1.5 mm) wire, using the 3.85mm mandrel as the form.

3 Solder together each individual large circular link. You're not assembling them yet; you're just closing their ends. Then string the links together on a spare piece of silver wire, and pickle, rinse, and dry them.

○ You will need 18 large round links with an inside diameter of 12.5 mm, and 18 small round links with an inside diameter of 3.85 mm to produce a chain that is 15 ¾ inches (40 cm) long.

4 Using the 3.25mm mandrel, shape each large circular link into an oval.

5 Working on one link at a time, grasp each end of an oval in the jaws of your flat-nose pliers. Make sure that you have the same amount of link in the jaws of the pliers at both ends. Then, holding the pliers firmly, give the link a full turn, as shown in figure 1. Twist the remaining large links the same way.

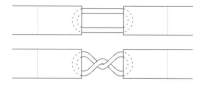

Figure 1

6 You'll make the fastener for this chain from one of the links that you just twisted. Choose a link and start by soldering it together at its middle—the point where it crosses over itself. This will stabilize the junction.

7 On the side of the link without the solder joint, use your jeweler's saw to cut through the link very near its center. (See figure 2.) Use your round-nose pliers to open the cut end of the link. Then file off the small stub that's left at the center of the link.

Figure 2

8 Form a small bead on the open end of the link. (See pages 29 through 30.)

9 With your round-nose pliers, bend the open end back to its original shape; however, this time, leave a small gap between the beaded end and the rest of the link. (See figure 3.) Adjust this gap so that the final link—the 9mm jump ring—will just slip through it with a little pressure.

Figure 3

10 Starting with the fastener that you just made, assemble the chain by alternating between twisted links and circular links. Then solder the small links closed.

11 The final link in the chain should be a small circular link; loop the 9mm jump ring through it, and solder the jump ring closed. Then pickle and rinse the chain.

12 You can leave the small links as they are, or you can use your flat-nose pliers to gently squeeze them into slight ovals. Before you shape the links, though, turn each one so that its solder joint will be hidden by the adjoining link. I find that this chain looks best if the small links end up approximately the same width as the twisted links.

13 Give the whole chain a light sanding, paying particular attention to the fastener. Wash the chain with a little dish soap and rinse with water to remove any grit. Then finish by polishing it in your tumbler.

A Jeweler's Favorite

THIS DESIGN GETS ITS NAME BECAUSE
SUPPOSEDLY IT SHOWS OFF A JEWELER'S SKILLS.
ACTUALLY, THE CHAIN IS QUITE EASY TO MAKE.

*You will need 59 pieces of silver wire, each about ⅞ inch (2.2 cm) long, to
produce a chain that is 15¾ inches (40 cm) long.*

MATERIALS & TOOLS

- 4½ feet (1.4 m) of 16-gauge (1.25 mm) round silver wire
- 9mm jump ring made from 16-gauge (1.25 mm) round silver wire
- 3.25mm round mandrel
- 400-grit sanding stick
- 800-grit sanding stick

1 Start by cutting 59 pieces of 16-gauge (1.25 mm) wire, each about ⅞ inch (2.2 cm) long. You'll use 58 of these pieces to make 29 links. The remaining piece will form half of the chain's fastener.

2 File the ends of each piece flat, removing about 1/32 inch (1 mm) of material from each end. (The pieces should be about ¾ inch [2 cm] long after you've filed them.) Then round the ends slightly by filing a slight bevel around each end to remove the sharp edge. (See figure 1.) Then finish with a quick pass of the 400-grit sanding stick.

3 Using figure 2 as a guide, bend each piece around the 3.25mm mandrel. Start by bending the piece into a V-shape with your fingers; then finish shaping it with flat-nose pliers. The ends of each teardrop should touch.

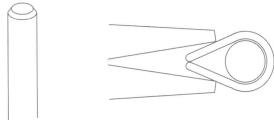

Figure 2

Figure 1

89

4 Each link in the chain is formed from two teardrops. To assemble the first link, start by grasping each piece in a pair of flat nose pliers, holding one piece horizontally and the other piece vertically, with their ends facing each other. (See figure 3.) Then push the links together where the ends meet until the pieces slide one into the other. You may have to wiggle them slightly to get them to slide together.

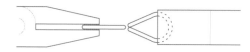

Figure 3

5 The easiest way to assemble this chain is to link all of the teardrop shapes together before any of them are soldered. To add a piece to the chain, turn the teardrop shape on one end of the chain so that you access the point where the ends meet. Slide another teardrop piece through this end piece, as described in step 4. Continue adding pieces in this fashion until you have linked all of the teardrop-shaped pieces together.

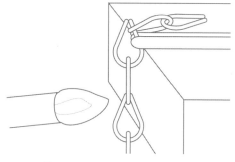

Figure 4

Arrange the shapes into pairs such that the pointed ends of the teardrops are together, giving each pair of pieces the appearance of an hourglass.

6 After you've assembled all of the teardrops (including number 59, which will be half of the fastener you make, starting with step 8), solder the links closed. To do this, grip one end of the chain in your third-hand cross-locking tweezers and drape the rest of it over your soldering block, as shown in figure 4. The weight of the chain itself will keep the links in the proper position.

7 There are four small areas on each link where the ends of each teardrop shape forming the link come together. Apply flux, and place a small snippet of solder on top of the joint area. Heat the joint until the solder melts and flows into the joint area. Cool the link in water, and examine it to make sure all four wires soldered. You'll probably have to solder most of the joints twice; at least one of the ends of these teardrop links always seems to resist your first attempt at soldering it. For the second pass, turn the link so that the unsoldered wire or wires face the torch flame. Flux the joint, and add another snippet of solder before heating the joint again. Solder all the teardrops this way.

8 To make the other part of the fastener for this chain, start by cutting a 1⅛-inch (3 cm) piece from the 16-gauge (1.25 mm) wire. Draw a bead on one end of the piece. (See pages 29 through 30.)

9 Use your round-nose pliers to bend the beaded end of the wire to a 90° angle. Then bend the piece around the 3.25mm mandrel, as shown in figure 5, making sure to leave a gap between the ends.

Figure 5

10 Butt-solder the fastener piece perpendicular to the teardrop, or half link, at the end of the chain. Then loop a 9mm jump ring through the last link on the other end. Solder the jump ring closed.

11 Pickle, rinse, and dry the chain.

12 To remove the tool marks on this chain, you'll need to sand each link individually, on all four wires at the central junction. It will only take a couple of swipes with the thin edge of a 400-grit sanding stick, and a few more with an 800-grit sanding stick. The most difficult part is finding a way to hold the links in position. I find that pulling the chain tight over the end of my thumb works best.

13 After you're done sanding, wash and rinse the chain. Then polish it in your tumbler.

○ *You will need 13 figure-eight links, 27 circular links with an inside diameter of 2 mm, and 12 circular links with an inside diameter of 3.25 mm to make a chain that is 15¾ inches (40 cm) long.*

MATERIALS & TOOLS

- 4 feet (1.25 m) of 16-gauge (1.25 mm) round silver wire
- 7.5mm jump ring made from 16-gauge (1.25 mm) round silver wire
- Piece of scrap wood, ¼ inch thick and at least 2 inches by 3 inches (1 cm thick and at least 5 cm by 8 cm)
- Spare piece of silver wire
- Round needle file
- Fine-tipped marker
- 1.25mm mandrel
- 5mm mandrel
- 3.25mm mandrel
- 2.5mm mandrel
- 2mm mandrel
- 400-grit sanding stick
- 800-grit sanding stick

figure-Eight Loops

THIS GRACEFUL AND UNUSUAL CHAIN ISN'T AS DIFFICULT TO MAKE AS IT MIGHT LOOK. IT'S MADE FROM THREE DIFFERENT TYPES OF LINKS: FIGURE EIGHTS WITH DECORATIVE LOOPS, ROUND RINGS SOLDERED TO BOTH ENDS OF EACH FIGURE EIGHT, AND SLIGHTLY OVAL LINKS THAT LOOP THROUGH THE SMALL RINGS TO CONNECT THE FIGURE-EIGHT LINKS. WIDE CHAINS OF THIS SORT OFTEN LOOK BETTER IF THEY'RE MADE A BIT LONGER. YOU MAY WANT TO MAKE A FEW EXTRA LINKS SO YOU CAN EXTEND THE CHAIN IF NECESSARY.

1 Cut 14 pieces of 16-gauge (1.25 mm) wire, each just a little more than 2⁷/₁₆ inches (6.2 cm) long. File the ends of the pieces flat, reducing each one to a length of 2⁵/₁₆ inches (6 cm).

2 You'll file a circular groove, rather like a saddle, at both ends of each 2⁵/₁₆-inch-long (6 cm) piece with a round needle file. The tricky part of this procedure is finding a way to hold the wire steady while you file it. Here's how I do it: File a small, V-shaped notch in the face of your piece of scrap wood, right at the wood's upper edge. Clamp the wood in your vice, with the notch facing towards you. Grasp one of the lengths of wire in your flat-nose pliers, and hold it against the notch in the scrap wood, bracing the pliers' tip against the wood. Figure 1 shows how the setup should look.

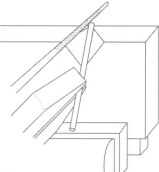

Figure 1

3 To file the end grooves, start by using a hand file to make a small flat spot on the edge of one end of one of the wire pieces. This flat spot will keep the needle file from slipping around the wire. Bracing the wire against the notch in the wood, use the round needle file to make a saddle-shaped groove in the wire's end. Repeat at the other end of the wire piece, making sure that the grooves are oriented in the same direction. (See figure 2.) Then give the ends of each piece a quick pass with the 400-grit sanding stick to remove any burrs.

Figure 2

4 On each piece of wire, carefully measure in $3/16$ inch (5 mm) from both ends and mark these points with your fine-tipped marker. Using the marks as a guide, insert $3/16$ inch (5 mm) of one of the pieces in the jaws of your flat-

nose pliers. Bend the end, as shown in figure 3. (Note how the groove is positioned in the pliers.) Repeat on the opposite end, bending in the other direction to form the piece into an elongated Z-shape. Bend all of the wire pieces this way.

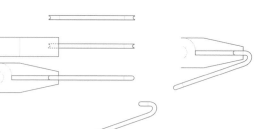

Figure 3

5 Grip the 1.25mm mandrel vertically in your vise. Using your flat-nose pliers, tightly curl the end of one of the wire pieces around the mandrel. The goal is to curl the wire around the mandrel as tightly as possible so that the groove filed in the end straddles the main length of wire, as shown in figure 4. The end of the wire should meet the main length at a right angle, as shown. Curl the other end in the same manner. The piece should now be about 2 inches (5 cm) long. Shape the other wire pieces the same way. At this point, the pieces probably won't be quite straight anymore, but don't worry about straightening them until after you've soldered the end loops closed in the next step; otherwise, you might disturb the tight fit you just made where the wire ends meet the main wire lengths.

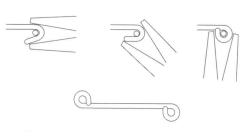

Figure 4

6 To solder the end loops closed, grip one of the pieces in your third-hand cross-locking tweezers. Apply soldering flux and a snippet of solder to the joint of each loop; then heat with your torch. Cool in some water and repeat with the other pieces.

7 Straighten the pieces with your flat-nose pliers. Sand off any tool marks with the 400-grit sanding stick, followed by a few passes with the 800-grit sanding stick.

8 Find and mark the center of each of the wire pieces. Then measure out $1/16$ inch (1.5 mm) from both sides of the center, and mark these points. These marks will guide you as you bend the pieces into figure eights.

9 Using figure 5 as a guide, bend the ends of each piece into figure-eight loops around the 5mm mandrel. The best way to do this is to hold the small, decorative circle at one end of the wire in flat-nose pliers, while grasping the other end of the wire in your fingers. As figure 5 shows, the end of each loop should touch the main length of wire at the $1/16$-inch (1.5 mm) mark farthest from it; make sure that the wires touch at these contact points.

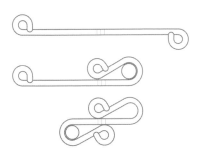

Figure 5

10 Select one figure-eight link to become your connector hook. Place it on your soldering block, apply flux and solder to one side of the figure eight (the other side will stay open to act as a hook), and heat the joint with your torch. After soldering, cool the piece in some water.

11 Solder closed both ends of all the other figure-eight links. Then pickle and rinse all the pieces. Set aside the fastener piece for now.

12 Straighten out the figure eight pieces, using two pairs of flat-nose pliers. Then sand off any tool marks.

13 Form and cut the 27 small circular rings that attach to the ends of the figure eights from the 16-gauge (1.25 mm) wire, using the 2mm mandrel as the form.

14 Solder closed each individual small, circular ring. (You're not assembling them, just closing their ends.) Then string them together on a spare piece of silver wire and pickle, rinse, and dry them.

15 File a flat spot on each small circular ring, right across the solder joint. File a similar spot on the ends of the figure-eight links, where you'll attach the rings. The piece designated

to be the connector hook only gets a ring, and therefore a flat spot, on the end that's soldered closed. I usually solder this piece first.

16 Solder the rings to the figure-eight links one at a time. The best way to do this is to place a figure eight on top of your soldering block. Position one of the small rings against one end of the figure eight, making sure to align the flat spots you filed in step 15. Apply a little flux to the joint. (Figure 6 shows how the setup should look.) Then, before placing a snippet of solder, heat the joint a little with your torch to dry the flux. This will cause the pieces to stick together. Place a snippet of solder on the joint, and solder the pieces together. Cool the piece in water; then repeat the operation on the other end. Solder a ring to each end of all the figure eights, except the connector.

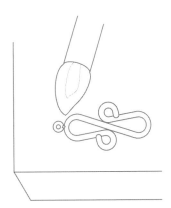

Figure 6

17 String together the figure eights on a spare piece of silver wire. Then pickle and rinse them.

18 The figure-eight links are joined together by looping a circular link through the rings at the ends of the figure eights. Form and cut 12 circular links from the 16-gauge (1.25 mm) wire, using the 3.25mm mandrel as the form.

19 Starting with the connector piece at one end, link the chain together, soldering the circular links as you go. Remember to mask the links that you're not soldering by draping the chain back over your soldering block. Keep in mind that the figure-eight links have a definite right-left orientation and should be arranged so that they all lie in the same direction. (See the project photo.)

20 Link a 7.5mm jump ring to the last circular loop at the other end of the chain and solder it closed. This will mate with the connecting figure eight.

21 Pickle, rinse, and dry the chain.

22 If you'd like to shape the connecting circular links into ovals (as shown in the project photo), you'll need to modify your 2.25mm mandrel by filing a flat spot on one of its ends. (See page 30 in chapter 1.) Then shape the links into ovals around it. The jump ring, however, should remain circular.

23 Sand the whole chain as usual. Then wash it with a little dish soap and rinse under water before polishing it in your tumbler.

Teardrop-Link Chain

This is a beautiful project for use with a pendant, and step 23 below will show you how to arrange the chain for this purpose. Constructing a teardrop-link chain is also excellent practice for making the similar, but more complex, Knotted-Link Chain on page 98.

☼ *You will need 23 teardrop links and 23 (or 25, if you're adding a pendant) circular links with an inside diameter of 3.25 mm, to make a chain that is 15¾ inches (40 cm) long.*

MATERIALS & TOOLS

- 4 feet (1.25 m) of 16-gauge (1.25 mm) round silver wire
- 7.5mm jump ring made from 16-gauge (1.25 mm) round silver wire (optional, see step 23)
- Fine-gauge binding wire made from iron
- 4.25mm round mandrel
- 3.25mm round mandrel
- 2.25mm round mandrel
- 2mm round mandrel
- Square needle file
- 400-grit sanding stick
- 800-grit sanding stick

1 Cut 23 straight pieces, each 1⅛ inches (3 cm) long, from the 16-gauge (1.25 mm) wire. Then cut one piece that's 2 inches (5 cm) long; you'll use this longer piece to make a connector hook for fastening the chain.

2 Form one of the 1⅛-inch (3 cm) pieces into a teardrop shape by bending it around the 4.25mm mandrel with your fingers. Then squeeze the ends with flat-nose pliers so that the piece has a teardrop shape around the mandrel with straight legs. (See figure 1.) Using the pliers, adjust the legs of the piece so that they lie parallel to each other and touch along their length. If the link is particularly stubborn, use fine-gauge binding wire made from iron to hold the legs together.

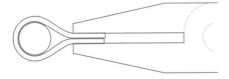

Figure 1

3 Repeat step 2 with the other 1⅛-inch (3 cm) pieces and with the 2-inch (5 cm) piece. The 2-inch (5 cm) piece will have longer legs and will probably require binding wire in a couple of places to hold the legs together.

4 Solder together the legs of the connector piece. To do this, place it on your soldering block. Apply flux along the entire length of the legs. Place a snippet of solder that's about 1/16-inch square (1.5 mm square) across the legs, approximately 3/16 inch (5 mm) from their ends. Place another 1/16-inch-square snippet across the legs about 3/16 inch from where they meet the teardrop loop. Apply heat along the length of the legs with your torch. The solder should run along the groove between the legs to solder the whole length together.

Remove the binding wire, pickle the piece, and set it aside until step 18.

5 Next, solder together the legs of the remaining teardrop pieces. These will require only a single piece of solder placed near the ends of the legs. The job will go faster if you prepare several pieces at a time and place them on top of your soldering block. Then move the torch from one to the next, soldering each as you go.

6 After you've soldered all the pieces, remove and discard any binding wire. Then string the teardrops together on some spare silver wire and pickle them. Rinse and dry them.

7 Sand off the tool marks you may have made while shaping the teardrops. These will mostly be in the area where the legs meet the pointed end of the teardrop shape. To reach this area, wrap a small piece of 400-grit sandpaper around the 4.25mm mandrel. Repeat the procedure, using 800-grit sandpaper.

8 The legs of each teardrop mate with a small circular link. A larger circular link loops through each of these mating links and the teardrop-end of the next teardrop to string together the necklace. Make the 23 small circular links (plus a few spares) from the 16-gauge (1.25 mm) wire, using the 2mm mandrel as the form. Don't worry about de-burring the links as you normally would; you'll file the cut ends in the following steps.

9 Figure 2 shows how the ends of a teardrop's legs fit into a V-shaped notch at the cut of a small circular mating link. To make this fit, you'll need to file the ends of the teardrops' legs, as well as the matching notch in the circular link. Start with the teardrops. Use a pair of diagonal cutters to trim the legs of each teardrop so that the link is ½ inch (13 mm) long. Run a hand file across the ends of the legs to remove the burr left by the side cutters. Then grasp the teardrop link in your flat-nose pliers so that the link is flat. You should be gripping the link by its face, not its edges; the teardrop portion of the link should be facing the pliers' handles, and the legs should be protruding from the pliers' jaws. File the legs to a knife point. Each leg should end up with an angle of about 45°; however, it's better to under-file at this point than to over-file. You can always touch up the legs after you've filed matching notches in the mating links.

Figure 2

10 Repeat step 9 on all the teardrops, with the exception of the larger one that's destined to become the connector hook.

11 Next, you need to file the matching groove in each of the small circular links that you made in step 8. Start by twisting a link closed, so that its ends touch and line up properly. (Note, however, that these links won't be soldered closed.) Then grasp the link in your flat-nose pliers so that the link is flat and its joint protrudes from the pliers' jaws. Use your hand file to make a small flat spot across the joint. (You'll be filing the groove with the edge of a square needle file, and without the flat spot, the file tends to slip along the links' sides.) Use the corner edge of your square needle file to cut the V-shaped groove at the link's joint. As you're filing, check the groove frequently to make sure that it's even on both sides.

12 Repeat step 11 on several more of the circular mating rings until you've filed one with a groove that's as good and as even as you can make it. (If you can create this groove on the first link you try, that's even better!) You'll use this model groove as a template for finishing the shaping of the legs of the teardrop links.

13 To check the fit, hold the leg end of one of the teardrop links against the groove in your model circular mating ring, as shown in figure 2. Touch up the filing of the legs of the teardrop link so that they match the groove as closely as possible. Use this same circular link as a template to touch up the filing on the rest of the teardrop links.

14 Select one of the teardrop links to use as a template, and file mating grooves in the remaining circular mating rings.

15 The circular links now need to be soldered onto the ends of the teardrop links. Select a teardrop link and a circular mating ring with a V groove and check the fit. If necessary, touch up the angles of the filing. Rinse off any silver sawdust by swishing the links in a container of water.

16 Position the teardrop link so that its angled legs protrude over the edge of your soldering block. Hold it in position by placing a heavy washer or some other weight on top of it. Grasp the circular mating ring in third-hand tweezers, and position it so that it mates with the end of the teardrop link. (See figure 3.) Add flux and place a 1/16-inch-square (1.5 mm) snippet of solder on the area of the joint. Heat the pieces from below. Both sides of the V-shaped joint should solder at the same time. However, if one side doesn't solder properly, don't move the tweezers or the link! Doing so will result in the link moving when you reheat the joint, and necessitate refiling both pieces to clean off the old solder. Instead, squeeze a few drops of water onto the joint area to cool it. Then add more flux and another small snippet of solder on the part that didn't solder the first time. Heat the pieces again from below.

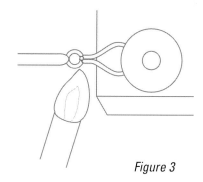

Figure 3

17 Repeat step 16 to solder the remaining teardrops and their mating circular rings. Then pickle, rinse, and dry all the pieces.

18 Make the connector hook from the teardrop piece you set aside in step 4. The process for making this hook is almost identical to the procedure for making a Simple Hook fastener (page 107), and you may want to refer to that fastener's illustrations for clarity. Start by filing the ends of the teardrop's legs round and smooth. Use your round-nose pliers to bend a slight angle in the last 1/8 inch (2 or 3 mm) at the legs' ends. Then shape the legs into a hook around the 3.25mm mandrel.

19 Fix any discrepancies in the joints and remove any tool marks from the connector and teardrop pieces you've made so far. If there are any large or major tool marks, you can file these away. However, a few passes with a 400-grit sanding stick, followed by a few more with an 800-grit sanding stick are usually sufficient.

20 Form and cut 23 circular links (or 25, if you plan to hang a pendant from the finished chain) from the 16-gauge (1.25 mm) wire, using the 3.25mm mandrel as the form.

21 Using the project photo as a guide, begin to assemble the chain. You'll assemble it in two lengths. Start with the connector hook you completed in step 18; using one of the larger circular rings (made in step 20), loop this through the fat end of the connector link and onto the small end of a teardrop shape. Twist the link closed. Continue adding teardrop links to the end of the chain in this way until you've used 11 teardrop links, in addition to the fastener.

22 Use the remaining 12 teardrops and associated large circular links to assemble a second length of chain.

23 If you're going to hang a pendant from this chain, arrange the two lengths so that the links point in opposite directions. (See figure 4.) Join the lengths together with three of the large circular links, assembling the pieces as shown in figure 4. In this configuration, the connector hook will be at one end of the chain, but the other end will only have one of the small circular rings. Add a 7.5mm jump ring to this end for the connector hook to mate with, and solder it closed.

Figure 4

24 If you're not going to use this chain for hanging a pendant, simply join the two lengths, links all pointing in the same direction, with one of the large circular links from step 20. The connector hook will mate with the last large circular link on the other end of the chain.

25 Solder all of the large circular links closed. Then pickle, rinse, and dry the chain.

26 To shape the large circular links that connect the teardrops into ovals (as shown in the project photo), file a flat spot on one end of your 2.25mm mandrel. (See page 30.) Then shape the large circular links into ovals around it. If you've arranged the chain to hold a pendant, as in step 23, leave the central link of the group of three you added in that step circular. It's the link from which you will suspend the pendant.

27 Sand the chain in the usual manner; then wash, rinse, and tumble polish it.

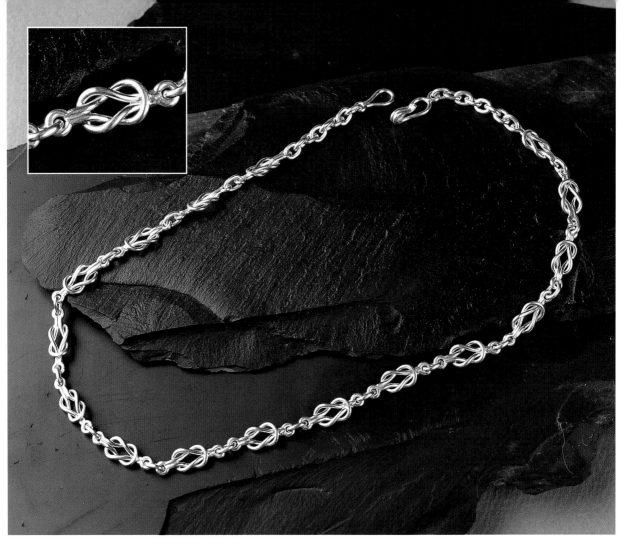

☼ *You will need 16 knotted links and 17 circular links with an inside diameter of 3.85 mm to produce a chain that is 15¾ inches (40 cm) long.*

Knotted-Link Chain

THE LINKS IN THIS CHAIN LOOK AS THOUGH THEY'RE MADE FROM WIRE THAT HAS BEEN TIED IN SQUARE KNOTS. OF COURSE, THIS REALLY ISN'T HOW THEY'RE CONSTRUCTED! THERE ARE ACTUALLY QUITE A FEW SEPARATE STEPS INVOLVED IN MAKING THESE LINKS. IN FACT, IN TERMS OF CONSTRUCTION, THIS IS PROBABLY THE MOST COMPLICATED CHAIN IN THE BOOK.

YOU CAN ADD LENGTH TO THIS CHAIN VERY EASILY BY ADDING MORE 3.85MM OVAL LINKS BETWEEN THE FASTENER PIECES AND THE LAST KNOTTED LINK AT EACH END OF THE CHAIN. THESE ADDITIONAL OVAL LINKS ARE ASSEMBLED JUST LIKE A BASIC TRACE CHAIN. (SEE PAGE 35.)

MATERIALS & TOOLS

- 6½ feet (2 m) of 14-gauge (1.5 mm) round silver wire
- Fine-gauge binding wire made of iron
- 5mm round mandrel
- 2mm round mandrel
- 2.25mm round mandrel with a flat spot filed on one end (see step 27)
- 3.85mm round mandrel
- 400-grit sanding stick
- 800-grit sanding stick

1 Begin by cutting one straight piece 2⅜ inch (6 cm) long and 33 straight pieces 1⁹⁄₁₆ inch (4 cm) long from the 14-gauge (1.5 mm) wire. You'll use the 2⅜-inch (6 cm) piece and one of the 1⁹⁄₁₆-inch (4 cm) pieces to make the connector. The other 32 pieces will be used to form 16 knotted links.

2 Form one of the 1⁹⁄₁₆-inch (4 cm) pieces into a teardrop shape by bending it around the 5mm mandrel with your fingers. Then use your flat-nose pliers to squeeze the piece's ends so it has a teardrop shape around the mandrel with straight legs. (See figure 1.) Using the pliers, adjust the legs of the piece so that they lie parallel to each other and touch along their length. If you need to, use fine-gauge binding wire made from iron to hold the legs together.

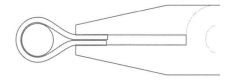

Figure 1

3 Repeat step 2 with the 32 other 1⁹⁄₁₆ inch (4 cm) pieces.

4 Solder together the legs of each teardrop piece. Start by applying flux along the entire length of the legs. Then place an approximately ¹⁄₁₆-inch-square (1.5 mm-square) snippet of solder across the legs, about ³⁄₁₆ inch

(5 mm) from their ends. Apply heat along the length of the legs with your torch. The solder should run along the groove between the legs to solder the whole length together. Speed up the process by preparing several pieces at once. Place them on top of your soldering block; then move the torch from one piece to the next, soldering each as you go.

5 String all the teardrops together on a spare piece of silver wire, and pickle them. (If you used binding wire to hold the legs together, remove and discard it before pickling the teardrops.) Rinse and dry all the pieces, and set one aside until step 23 for use with the connector piece in the fastener.

6 Sand off any tool marks, using the 5mm mandrel wrapped in 400-grit sandpaper. Then repeat with 800-grit sandpaper.

7 Before "tying" the teardrops into knots, gently bend each one. Start by grasping the lower end of the loop portion of one of the teardrops in a pair of flat-nose pliers. Grasp most of the rest of the piece in another pair. Using figure 2 as a guide, bend the link slightly upward. Then move the pair of pliers holding the legs a little further back and bend some more. Finish the bend, holding just the leg portion of the piece. The result should be a gentle curve of the loop area, with the legs still straight and pointing upwards at an angle of about 45°, as shown in figure 3. Repeat on the other 31 teardrop link pieces.

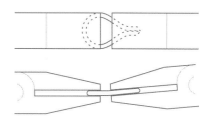

Figure 2

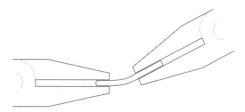

Figure 3

8 To form the knot shapes, begin by sliding two of the teardrop pieces together, as shown in figure 4. At this point, the legs of each teardrop are offset from each other and the pieces slide easily apart. Using two pairs of flat-nose pliers, grasp the legs of each teardrop and pull the pieces together tightly. Then, move one pair of pliers so that its jaws hold the pieces together. At the other end of the knot, grasp the teardrop so that the round part of its loop and legs are inside the

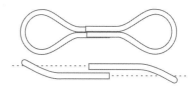

Figure 4

jaws of your flat-nose pliers; squeeze these pliers to bend the legs around the loop a little. (See figure 5.) This will put the legs more in line with the link, and keep the pieces from slipping apart. Repeat at the other end of the knot. The two teardrops in the knotted link should now hold together firmly, and the legs of each one should be in line with the link as a whole. (See figure 6.) Repeat this procedure to make 16 knotted links.

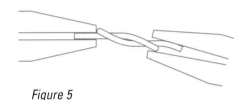

Figure 5

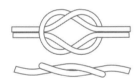

Figure 6

9 Solder each knotted link. Place one on your soldering block. Apply flux to the area on one side of the knot where the loop of one teardrop crosses over the legs of the other teardrop. Position an approximately 1/16-inch-square (1.5 mm-square) snippet of solder standing up against the loop, as shown in figure 7. Heat the piece from above with your torch.

Usually, both of the leg pieces will get soldered to the loop at the same time; however, you can resolder if necessary to make sure that both wires of the legs are soldered to the crossover loop. Turn the link over, and repeat this operation at the other end of the knot.

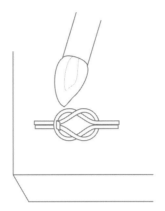

Figure 7

10 Repeat step 9 to solder all of the knotted links. Then pickle, rinse, and dry them.

11 A small circular link mates with the legs at each end of each knotted link. These links act as connectors for larger oval links that join the knots into a chain. Form and cut 34 of these small circular links (plus a few spares) from 14-gauge (1.5 mm) wire, using the 2mm mandrel as the form. Don't worry about de-burring the links; you'll file their ends later.

12 Figure 8 shows how the legs at both ends of each knotted link mate with the small circular links. Note that the ends of the legs are filed to a sharp point that fits into a V-shaped groove filed in the mating circular link.

Figure 8

13 Use diagonal cutters to trim the legs of the two teardrops that form each knotted link. About 5/64 inch (2 mm) of the legs should remain protruding over the adjacent loop. (See figure 9.) Smooth the cut ends with a hand file, but don't worry about making them completely flat.

Figure 9

14 Grasp one of the knotted links with your flat-nose pliers so that just the ends of the legs on one side protrude from the jaws. (It's important to hold the knot deep in your pliers this way so that the pliers' ends will protect the rounded shoulder of the link from an accidental brush with your file.) File the legs' ends to a knife edge, as shown in figure 8. Aim for a 45° angle, but avoid creating a long, narrow point. At this stage, it's better to have the ends remain a more blunt shape. Later, you can adjust the shape to fit the groove in the mating small circular link.

15 Reverse the link's position in your pliers and file the ends of the legs on the other side the same way. Repeat on the remaining knotted links.

16 File mating V-shaped grooves in 32 of the 34 small circular links. (You'll use the two remaining links when making the fastener in steps 23 and 24.) Start by twisting a link closed, so that its ends touch and line up properly. Then grasp the link in your flat-nose pliers so that the link is flat and its joint protrudes from the pliers' jaws. File a small flat spot across the joint. Cut the V-shaped groove at the link's joint with the corner of your square needle file. (See figure 8.) As you're filing, check the groove frequently to make sure that it's even on both sides. Continue filing until the groove is almost all the way through the joint.

17 Repeat step 16 on several more of the circular mating rings until you've filed one with a groove that's as good and as even as you can make it. In the next step, you'll use this model groove as a template for finishing the shaping of the legs of the knotted links.

18 Hold the leg end of one of the links against the groove in your model circular mating ring to check the fit. Touch up the filing on the legs of the knotted link so that they match the groove as closely as possible. Check the filing on the legs at the other end of the knot. Then use this same circular link as a template to touch up the filing on the rest of the knotted links.

19 Select one of the knotted links to use as a template. Then file mating grooves in the remaining circular mating rings, using the knotted-link template to get the grooves as even as possible.

20 The circular links now need to be soldered onto the ends of the knotted links. Select a knotted link and two circular mating rings. Check the fit of each groove against the ends of the knot's legs. If necessary, touch up the angles of the filing. Rinse off any silver sawdust by swishing the links in a container of water.

21 Position the knotted link so that the angled legs at one end protrude over the edge of your soldering block. Hold it in position by placing a heavy washer or some other weight on top of it. Grasp one of the circular mating rings in third-hand cross-locking tweezers, and position it so that it mates with the end of the knotted link. Add flux and an approximately $1/16$-inch-square (1.5 mm-square) snippet of solder on the area of the joint. Heat the pieces from below. Both sides of the V-shaped joint should solder at the same time. However, if one side doesn't, don't move the tweezers or the link! Doing so will probably result in the link moving when you reheat the joint. This will necessitate refiling both pieces to clean off the old solder. Instead, squeeze a few drops of water onto the joint area to cool it. Then add more flux and another solder snippet on the

part that didn't solder the first time. Heat the pieces again from below.

22 Reverse the knotted link and solder the other circular mating ring to the other end. Repeat on the remaining knotted links.

23 Make the connector portion of the fastener from the teardrop you set aside in step 5 and one of links from step 16. Start by trimming the ends of the teardrop's legs so that the whole piece is about $9/16$ inch (14 mm) long. File the ends of the legs to a knife edge, just as you did on the ends of the legs on the knotted links. File a matching V-shaped groove in the small circular link. Solder the circular link to the ends of the legs.

24 The hook portion of this chain's fastener is very similar to the Simple Hook, and you may find it useful to review the instructions and illustrations for that fastener on page 107. Start by shaping the $2^3/8$-inch-long(6 cm) piece of 14-gauge (1.5 mm) silver wire into a teardrop shape around the 5mm mandrel. Solder together the legs of the teardrop, as described in step 4. Round the ends of the legs with a file; then use your round-nose pliers to bend about $1/8$ inch (2 to 3 mm) of the legs down at a slight angle. Then bend the legs into a hook shape around the 3.85mm mandrel. Adjust the gap in the hook so that the connector piece you made in step 23 slips on to it with a little pressure. Finish the fastener by butt-soldering the remaining small circular link to the fat end of the teardrop.

24 Pickle, rinse, and dry the knotted links and the fastener pieces. Then check all of the links, and touch up any discrepancies in their joints with a 400-grit sanding stick. Finish with a few more passes with your 800-grit sanding stick.

25 Form and cut 17 circular links (plus a few spares) from the 14-gauge (1.5 mm) wire, using the 3.85mm mandrel as the form. Clean and de-burr the links.

26 Join the knotted links and the fastener pieces into a chain by linking them together with the 3.85mm circular links. The knotted links have a definite right-left orientation; be careful to assemble them all in the same direction. After you've assembled the whole chain, solder the joints of the 3.85mm circular links. Then pickle, rinse, and dry the chain.

27 The 3.85mm links that join the chain together are shaped into slight ovals. To do this, you'll need to file a flat spot almost halfway through your 2.25mm mandrel. Then slip each 3.85mm link over the mandrel and squeeze it into an oval, making sure that the solder joint is at one end of the link.

28 Sand the whole chain smooth in the usual manner. Then wash it with a little soap and water before polishing it in the tumbler.

Scalloped Necklace

The "links" in this rather elegant necklace are made in a different way from any of the others in this book. Nevertheless, this project still qualifies as a chain—and one of my wife's favorites, at that! The Scalloped Necklace needs no pendants or other additions: It is complete by itself.

As with the other projects in this book, the instructions here will produce a chain that is 15¾ inches (40 cm) long. Due to the different nature of the links in this necklace, however, the calculations given on page 19 for adjusting a chain's length won't work here. The Design Tip on page 103 will tell you how to lengthen or shorten this chain.

- 10½ feet (3.25 m) of 14-gauge (1.5 mm) round silver wire
- 3½ feet (1.1 m) of 16-gauge (1.25 mm) round silver wire
- 7mm spring ring
- 7mm jump ring made from 16-gauge (1.25 mm) round silver wire
- 2mm round mandrel
- 3mm round mandrel
- 6.5mm round mandrel
- 8mm round mandrel
- 4-inch (10 cm) round mandrel (I used a short length of plastic pipe.)
- Square needle file
- 400-grit sanding stick
- 800-grit sanding stick

DESIGN TIP:

TO ADJUST THE LENGTH OF THIS CHAIN, ADD OR REMOVE LINKS FROM THE SECTIONS OF TRACE CHAIN THAT JOIN THE SCALLOPED LINKS TO THE FASTENER. YOU COULD ALSO CHANGE THE LENGTH OF THE "DUMBBELL" LINKS, BUT THIS IS MORE DIFFICULT AS IT TAKES SOME EXPERIMENTATION TO GET THE LENGTHS OF EACH PIECE IN THE THREE-LINK GROUPS PROPERLY PROPORTIONED.

1 The basic "link" in this chain begins as a kind of "dumbbell" shape—a straight piece of wire with a circular ring soldered to each end. The list that follows shows the length of the straight pieces you'll need. Cut these pieces about $\frac{3}{32}$ inch (2 mm) longer than indicated, because you'll lose about that much when you file their ends smooth.

- Two $\frac{5}{16}$-inch (8 mm) pieces
- Two $\frac{13}{32}$-inch (10 mm) pieces
- Two $\frac{1}{2}$-inch (13 mm) pieces
- Two $\frac{13}{16}$-inch (20 mm) pieces
- Two $\frac{7}{8}$-inch (22 mm) pieces
- Two $\frac{15}{16}$-inch (24 mm) pieces
- Two $1\frac{7}{16}$-inch (36 mm) pieces
- Two $1\frac{9}{16}$-inch (40 mm) pieces
- Two $1\frac{25}{32}$-inch (45 mm) pieces
- One $2\frac{9}{16}$-inch (65 mm) piece
- One $2\frac{23}{32}$-inch (69 mm) piece
- One 3-inch (76 mm) piece

2 File the ends of each wire length smooth, and remove any additional wire necessary to reduce the pieces to the specified lengths.

3 File both ends of each straight piece to a knife edge; the ideal angle is 45°.

4 Form and cut 42 circular links (plus a few spares) from the 14-gauge (1.5 mm) wire, using the 3mm mandrel as the form. Clean and de-burr these links.

5 Solder closed the ends of the circular links in the usual manner. Then pickle, rinse, and dry them.

6 Grasp one of the circular links in your flat-nose pliers so that its solder joint just protrudes from the jaws. Use your hand file to smooth a small flat spot across the solder joint; then cut a V-shaped groove about halfway through the joint with your square needle file. Check the groove often to make sure you're filing it even and straight. Cut grooves into the remaining circular links the same way.

7 Solder a circular link onto both ends of each of the straight pieces. Start by checking the groove in a circular link against the pointed end of a straight piece. Adjust the groove or the point as necessary. Then grasp the circular link in your third-hand cross-locking tweezers. Place the straight piece on your soldering block, with one of its pointed ends protruding over the edge. Weigh the straight piece down with a washer or some other piece of heavy hardware. Then fit the pointed end of the straight piece into the groove of the circular link. Apply flux and a solder snippet to the joint, and heat from below. Solder another circular link on the other end of the straight piece the same way. Repeat with the remaining straight pieces and circular links.

8 Pickle, rinse, and dry the "dumbbell" links. Then sand the areas around the solder joints of each one, first with the 400-grit sanding stick; then with the 800-grit sanding stick.

9 Use you fingers to bend each of the "dumbbell" links into a slight curve, using the 4-inch (10 cm) mandrel as a rough form. Note that the pieces aren't bent to conform to the curvature of the mandrel; each of the pieces is curved slightly differently, with the inner link of each group of three being less concave than the outer link. The basic guide is that the tip-to-tip length of each of the three pieces in a group should be the same. (See figure 1.)

10 Form and cut eight circular links (plus a few spares) from the 14-gauge (1.5 mm) wire, using the 6.5mm mandrel as the form. Clean and de-burr these links. These are the circular links that will join each group of three "dumbbell" links together.

11 Form and cut eight circular links (plus a few spares) from the 16-gauge (1.25 mm) wire, using the 8mm mandrel as the form. Clean and de-burr the links. These links will be made into two small lengths of trace chain to join the main portion of the necklace to the fastener.

12 Using figure 1 as a guide, assemble the chain. Solder all of the links closed and pickle the chain.

13 Shape the 8mm circular links into ovals around the 2mm mandrel.

14 Butt-solder the 7mm jump ring to the last oval link at one end of the chain, and pickle this area of the chain again.

15 Adjust the curvature of each of the links so that they form even and balanced three-link groups. This is probably the most important step in making this chain, so be patient and keep at it until the chain looks balanced and properly proportioned.

16 Touch up any noticeable tool marks with sandpaper or with your sanding sticks. Then wash the chain with a little soap and water before polishing it in the tumbler.

17 Loop the connector ring of the spring ring through the last oval link at the other end of the chain.

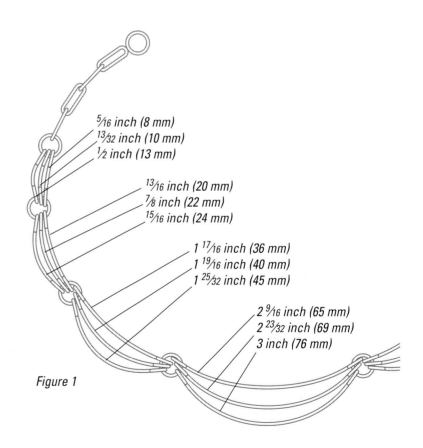

5/16 inch (8 mm)
13/32 inch (10 mm)
1/2 inch (13 mm)

13/16 inch (20 mm)
7/8 inch (22 mm)
15/16 inch (24 mm)

1 17/16 inch (36 mm)
1 19/16 inch (40 mm)
1 25/32 inch (45 mm)

2 9/16 inch (65 mm)
2 23/32 inch (69 mm)
3 inch (76 mm)

Figure 1

FINISHING TOUCHES:
"FASTENERS"

This chapter shows a few simple handmade findings you can use to fasten your chains. All of the designs are made from plain wire, with the same tools used for chain making. If you browse through a book on general silver-jewelry-making techniques, you'll probably find many other designs, including box clasps, cylinder clasps, sister hooks, and so on. While I encourage you to explore these other fasteners, most of them require techniques that are beyond the scope of this book. And, as you'll see in the pages that follow, you can make some very attractive findings with nothing more than silver wire.

The dimensions and wire sizes I've suggested in this chapter will result in fasteners appropriate for specific chains on which they're used in this book. However, you should feel free to alter any of these findings to match the specific chain of your choice. In general, almost any fastener can be used with almost any chain, although some fasteners (the End Caps with Hook and Ring on page 109, for instance) lend themselves to specific uses. Also, be sure to check out the fasteners suggested for the fancy link chains in chapter 6; these show a number of variations on the basic findings in this chapter.

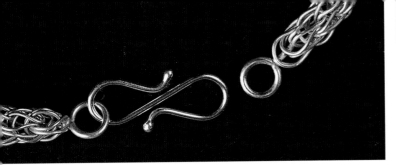

S-Hook Fastener

THIS SIMPLE, ATTRACTIVE FASTENER MATES VERY WELL WITH A VARIETY OF CHAIN STYLES. IT'S EASY TO USE, TOO, AND YOU CAN VARY HOW IT ATTACHES TO OTHER CHAINS AS YOU SEE FIT. YOU MAY, FOR EXAMPLE, SOLDER ONE OF THE LOOPS OF THE S-HOOK CLOSED TO PERMANENTLY ATTACH THE HOOK TO THE CHAIN AND PREVENT ITS POSSIBLE LOSS. IN THIS CASE, A SMALL JUMP RING IS OFTEN USED TO CONNECT THE SOLDERED SIDE OF THE LOOP TO THE CHAIN; A LARGER 6.5MM JUMP RING IS USED ON THE OTHER END OF THE CHAIN TO CONNECT TO THE OPEN LOOP OF THE S-HOOK.

MATERIALS & TOOLS

- 2³⁄₈ inches (6 cm) of 16-gauge (1.25 mm) round silver wire
- Fine-tipped marker
- Two 6.5mm jump rings made from 16-gauge (1.25 mm) round silver wire
- 5mm round mandrel

1 Start by drawing a bead on each end of the 2 ³⁄₈-inch (6 cm) length of wire. (See pages 29 through 30.) You'll lose about ⁵⁄₁₆ inch (2 mm) or so from the total length of the wire, depending on how large a bead you make.

2 Use your round-nose pliers to bend the ends of the wire 90° in opposite directions. The resulting piece should look like figure 1.

3 Use a fine-tipped marker to mark the exact center of the piece of wire. Then, measure out ³⁄₆₄ inch (1.5 mm) from each side of the center and mark these points. These marks will guide the bending of the loops and show the loops' contact points.

Figure 1

4 Use your fingers to bend the body of the wire around the 5 mm mandrel at each end to form the large loops. Then use your round-nose pliers to squeeze the angle of the ends with the beads against the appropriate ³⁄₆₄-inch (1.5 mm) mark. (See figure 2.) Note that the end of each loop contacts the mark closest to its end.

5 The wire will probably be a little soft after you heat it to form the beads. Open and close the gaps formed by the ends of the S-shape a few times to work harden the wire. You can do this by hand.

6 This particular fastener is shown in use on the Triple Loop-In-Loop Chain on page 81. To attach an S-hook to a triple loop-in-loop chain, solder a 6.5mm jump ring to each end of the chain. The S-hook simply hooks through each one of the jump rings to fasten the chain.

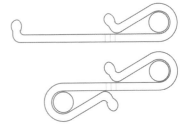

Figure 2

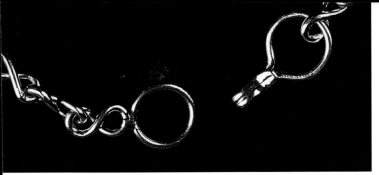

The Simple Hook

This fastener was made for the Simple Twisted-Link Chain on page 84. The fastener's exact shape and the way it connects to a chain offer a lot of room for variation. The projects in chapter 6 show several of these hook variations adapted to specific chains.

MATERIALS & TOOLS

- 4 inches (10 cm) of 18-gauge (1mm) round silver wire
- Fine-gauge binding wire made of iron
- 8mm jump ring made from 18-gauge (1 mm) round silver wire
- 6mm round mandrel
- 2mm round mandrel
- 400-grit sanding stick
- 800-grit sanding stick

1 Wind the 4-inch (10 cm) length of wire around the 6mm mandrel to form a sort of lollipop shape, as shown in figure 1. Use flat-nose pliers to squeeze the wire as close as possible around the mandrel, which will make the "lollipop" portion very round.

Figure 1

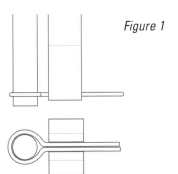

2 Twist a couple of short lengths of fine-gauge binding wire around the two straight legs that form the lollipop's "stick"; this will keep the legs in contact while you solder them together.

3 Set the piece on top of your soldering block, and apply flux for soldering to the legs. Place a snippet of solder between the legs, about ⅛ inch (3 mm) down from the bottom of the lollipop. Place another snippet between the legs, about ⅛ inch up from their ends.

4 Heat the legs of the piece evenly with your torch. The solder should flow through the groove between the legs, joining them together.

5 Remove the binding wire; then pickle, rinse, and dry the fastener.

6 Use your hand file to smooth the legs' ends; then sand the ends smooth with the sanding sticks.

7 Using figure 2 as a guide, bend a slight "lip" at the end of the legs with your round-nose pliers.

Figure 2

8 Use your round-nose pliers to shape the legs around the 2mm mandrel to form the basic hook. (See figure 3.)

Figure 3

9 Attach the hook part of the fastener by looping it through the last link at one end of the chain before soldering the link closed.

10 For the Simple Twisted-Link Chain (page 84), I butt-soldered the mating jump ring directly to the last link on the other end of the chain. This method makes the fastener easier to grip. However, you can simply loop the jump ring through the last link at the other end of the chain, and solder it closed.

Toggle Clasp

THIS POPULAR FINDING CAN BE USED AS A STANDARD, BEHIND-THE-NECK FASTENER ON MOST STYLES OF CHAINS. HOWEVER, IT'S ALSO PARTICULARLY GOOD FOR ATTACHING ITEMS SUCH AS POCKET-WATCH CHAINS TO BUTTONHOLES. I ALSO LIKE TO USE THEM AS DECORATIVE SHOWPIECES, ALONG WITH A SMALL BIT OF CHAIN AND A DANGLER OR CHARM OF SOME SORT. IN THIS CASE, THE CONNECTOR IS MOVED AROUND TO THE FRONT. YOU CAN ELABORATE ON TOGGLE CLASPS USED FOR THIS PURPOSE BY USING TWISTED SQUARE WIRE WITH SMALL DISKS SOLDERED ON THE ENDS FOR THE STRAIGHT PIECE, AND VARIOUS KINDS OF TEXTURED WIRE FOR THE CIRCULAR MATING RING.

MATERIALS TOOLS

- 7/8-inch (2.25 cm) straight piece of 18-gauge (1 mm) round silver wire
- Fine-tipped marker
- 5mm jump ring made from 18-gauge (1 mm) round silver wire
- 9mm jump ring made from 18-gauge (1 mm) round silver wire

1 Start by drawing a bead on each end of the 7/8-inch (2.25 cm) length of wire. (See pages 29 through 30.) You'll lose about 5/64 inch (2 mm) or so from the total length of the wire, depending on how large a bead you make.

2 Find and mark the center of the straight piece of wire with your fine-tipped marker. Then place the wire on top of your soldering block and position the cut end of the 5mm jump ring against the center mark. (See figure 1.)

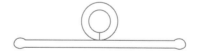

Figure 1

3 Apply soldering flux to the jump ring and the straight piece; then place a snippet of solder on their shared joint. Solder the pieces together; then pickle, rinse, and dry them.

4 To attach the straight piece to the end of your chain, simply loop the last link of the chain through the 5mm jump ring, and solder it closed.

5 You can solder the 9mm jump ring—the mating ring—directly to the other end of your chain; or you can solder a 5mm jump ring to the mating ring (as you soldered one to the straight piece in step 3). Then loop the last link of the chain's end through the smaller jump ring, and solder it closed.

End Caps with a Hook and Ring

SOME CHAINS THAT HAVE A ROUND SHAPE OFTEN LOOK BEST WITH END CAPS THAT HIDE THE WAY THEIR COMPLEX LINKINGS END. THE LOOP-IN-LOOP CHAINS IN CHAPTER 5, FOR EXAMPLE, MOVE FROM INTRICATE, MULTI-PIECE LINKAGES TO A SINGLE, RATHER BARE LINK AT EACH END. END CAPS WITH A HOOK AND RING WILL HIDE THIS PROBLEM EFFECTIVELY AND ADD AN EXTRA DECORATIVE FEATURE TO THE CHAIN. THE FASTENER SHOWN IN THE PROJECT PHOTO AND DESCRIBED HERE WAS DESIGNED SPECIFICALLY FOR THE DOUBLE LOOP-IN-LOOP CHAIN ON PAGE 78.

MATERIALS & TOOLS

- **16 inches (40 cm) of 18-gauge (1mm) round silver wire**
- **Fine-gauge binding wire made of iron**
- **5mm round mandrel**
- **Silver polish (optional, see step 18)**
- **Toothbrush (optional, see step 18)**

1 Place the 5mm mandrel vertically in the vise, trapping one end of the 18-gauge (1 mm) wire between the mandrel and the jaw of the vise.

2 Coil the wire around the mandrel for eight turns, keeping the turns as close together as possible. Remove the mandrel and the coil from the vise and snip off the end of the wire that was held in the vise. Then clip the coil from the length of the wire, leaving a stub of about ¾ inch (2 cm).

3 Repeat step 2 to make a second coil.

4 No matter how carefully you wound the coils around the mandrel in step 2, the turns probably won't all touch. To bring them together, feed two short lengths of fine-gauge binding wire through the center of each coil. Bring the turns of each coil together by twisting the ends of one of the pieces of binding wire together with flat-nose pliers. Repeat this with the other piece of binding wire on the other side of each coil, as shown in figure 1. Don't pull the binding wire

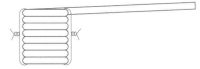

Figure 1

too tight, though; otherwise, you might distort the coils.

5 Dip a coil in the flux you use for annealing. Then rest it on top of the soldering block, and place two snippets of solder, each about ⅛-inch (3 mm) square, inside the coil. (Place a snippet near each end.)

6 Heat the coil with your torch until the solder melts; you'll be able to see the solder actually run around the grooves between the wire.

7 Cool the coil in some water; then check to make sure all the turns are soldered together. If they're not, dip the piece in annealing flux again, add one or two more snippets, and solder the coil again.

8 Repeat steps 5 through 7 with the second coil.

9 Remove and discard the binding wire; then pickle and rinse the coils.

10 On both coils, bend the ¾-inch (2 cm) stub across the top, as shown in figure 2.

Figure 2

11 Using figure 3 as a guide, form a ring on the end of one of the coils by winding the stub around the 5mm mandrel. Remove the mandrel; then trim the wire to length, apply annealing flux and a snippet of solder, and solder the ring closed.

Figure 3

12 Form a hook on the end of the other coil. To do this, start by trimming the straight stub to a length of about ½ inch (1.5 cm). (The stub should end up about three times as long as the width of the outside diameter of the coil.)

13 Draw a bead on the end of the trimmed stub, as described on pages 29 through 30 in chapter 1; then pickle and rinse it.

14 Form the hook by bending the stub around the 5mm mandrel with your round-nose pliers. Adjust the hook as needed to mate with the ring on the other coil.

15 Attach a coil to each end of your chain. To do this, start by crushing the chain ends slightly with flat-nose pliers. Then fit a coil over each end; the fit should be just tight enough to hold the pieces in place during soldering.

16 Dip each coil and the last few inches (cm) of the chain in annealing flux; then place two or three small snippets of solder inside each coil where the chain enters. You'll probably find that it's easiest to place the solder snippets with fine-tip tweezers.

17 Working with one end at a time, heat the pieces on your soldering block with your torch until the solder snippets melt. This will permanently fasten the end cap on the chain.

18 Pickle the ends of the chain; then polish the chain. If tumble polishing isn't recommended for that particular chain (as is the case with the loop-in-loop chains), you can clean the fastener and the chain ends with silver polish and a toothbrush.

Index of Subjects

Index of Projects